Pataphysica

Pataphysica

Edited by Cal Clements

Writers Club Press
San Jose New York Lincoln Shanghai

Pataphysica

Writers Club Press
an imprint of iUniverse, Inc.

For information address:
iUniverse, Inc.
5220 S. 16th St., Suite 200
Lincoln, NE 68512
www.iuniverse.com

ISBN: 0-595-23604-9

Printed in the United States of America

Contents

Preface

Cal Clements

In my quest to do nothing valuable in life, I decided to announce my willingness to entertain papers by anyone calling him or herself a pata-physician or pataphysicist. Given the scarcity of such creatures, I had hoped to tell the world that I was engaged as an editor of an esoteric scholarly journal while having nothing to edit. Furthermore, I had arranged with myself that I could be "on vacation" any day that an essay did not arrive in my mailbox. By mailbox, I mean the electronic mailbox in my computer, which I had programmed to emit the sound of a bell upon the arrival of new mail. Almost immediately I was disappointed. My computer's bell rang daily. Flocks of papers and scores of drafts presented themselves for my labor. Who knew there were so many cruel miners out there lusting for the dust of pataphysics? Of course I was terrible in my responses. Word must get out that I was an ogre under the bridge. Most importantly, I wanted to get back to my holiday. At this point, I would settle for a day off.

A project once started must be seen to its conclusion. Is this not a fundamental principle? It seemed so to my otherwise amoral sensibility.

I spent the better part of the year tending to my e-mail. A disaster. I had to figure out some way to depress the world's enthusiasm. I created needless technical problems, threw doubt upon my competence, and insisted upon an obscure style guide. My vision entertained the possibility of printing a one-page collection of sundry pataphysica in a microscopic font, thereby reducing proofreading, indexing, and printing needs. The page count, however, mounted. Far too many incandescent thoughts assailed me. All too often, I had to smile in wonder, rejoice in the fertility of the science, and include yet another contribution. The sheer profundity of the material turned my slapdash project into an immortal book.

In the end, I did select the smallest number of works possible. These are they.

With any group of items the first question is one of organization. How are they ordered? Do they ascend or descend in value or quantity of words? Do they introduce a theme along general lines and then develop it toward specific ends? Do they move chronologically (thereby mirroring the causation that is rumored to attend history)? Are they color-coded? My catalog of this year's work attempts to belie any organizing agenda. I left the essays in a heap. They are simply growing wild. Now when I read over the table of contents, I fill my lungs with the air of ethernity. In these moments, I feel as though I were a Heathcliff out on a stormy night, his back to a tree, his head craned back so as to look upon a dizzying array of tossing limbs. Try this yourself when you get to that page.

Meanwhile, let me provide what introductions cannot be avoided.

Pataphysics is nothing if not practical. It was always with an eye toward the working pataphysicist, the practicing pataphysician, that I selected the pieces. I had hoped to compile a set of field notes, a manual as useful as Hero's *Pneumatica*, or something to aid ongoing research into the rude machine. While there is nothing particularly diagrammatic among these papers, quite a few of the pieces work with sublime spatial dimensions. This is true of the opening piece, Scott Magelssen's meditation on Witkiewicz' Pure Form stage plays. Magelssen scours his travel diaries in order to compose a partial autobiography that elucidates the tension between physical and metaphysical spaces. Brian Parshall discusses Jarry's interest in the infinite sphere, "the circle without circumference." Throughout the article, he provides a depth that will charm historians. Pataphysicists will be pleased to discover David Daniels' 25 principles for working with "bodies in motion." The pataphysician MEZ offers hints for tuning the language of time machines. The relation between time-space-language is further explored in Chris Fritton's contribution. The layout of his text requires a special attention that may or may not be provided by our publisher. If all the letters do not line up properly, you may heap the blame squarely upon my shoulders (since I hired the least expensive publisher available). In a telegraphic letter to Jarry, Brisbane di Milo celebrates the space of the baseball diamond at a metaphysical and mythological level. Ric Royer shares some of the frustrations of working with higher space in an extract from the much larger *Zero's Wedding*. My own piece on Duchamp's infrathin must be regarded as a gift from the gods, a triumph in pataphysical scholarship, extremely insightful, and so forth. It explores elemental parallelism, hollow paper, shadows, nocturnal illumination, and molds *en route* the fourth dimension. As a result of these readings, you may expect your everyday practice of pataphysics to be enlightened, if only by some small degree.

Knowing that many of you are working on machines that generate laughter, I have included Anthony Enns' discussion of humor. Enns traces Jarry's own style of producing this outpouring not to Bergson, as is common, but to Nietzsche.

Included also are two essays on pataphysicians whom we wish to bring to your (renewed) attention. M. Alejandro Riberi's introduces Julio Cortázar. His essay has the distinction of having been written initially in Spanish, translated by the author into French, and then translated by Mark André Singer into English. Finally, we offer John van der Does' thoughts on Boris Vian. My first act of freedom, once this publication goes to press, will be to read *Blues for a Black Cat*. As it may take me some time to get through the tome, a few seasons may pass before the next edition of *Pataphysica* may be attempted. Please be patient and—in order to minimize the exercise of patience—read this edition very carefully.

While all errors in the text are wholly my fault, I have been immeasurably assisted by the keen eyes of Roumiana Velikova. She gave the first draft a thorough cleaning. If we groan less at the inconsistencies herein (although I hear some readers enjoy inconsistency) it is due to Roumiana's care and diligence. Further super-vision has been provided by Mark André Singer of the Mechanics' Institute of San Francisco and Professor Joan Copjec of The Center for the Study of Psychoanalysis and Culture at SUNY Buffalo.

I wish to also thank Gray Kochhar-Lindgren, Associate Professor of English at Central Michigan University, for helping me announce *Pataphysica* to the world. He may have done his job too well. Finally, two pataphysicans sent their books to me. Jerome McGann sent his sophisticated and lucid critical work, *Radiant Textuality*. David Daniels, whose work appears in this edition, sent *The Gates of Paradise*, which is a masterpiece of concrete poetry. Both books are excellent and heartily recommended. They have been added to my library.

Witkacy's Theory of Pure Form

Scott Magelssen

> Nothing beautiful can exist in this world! The human animal
> always interferes and spoils everything!
>
> —S.I. Witkiewicz

Who was Stanislaw Ignacy Witkiewicz, the early twentieth-century artist whose "Pure Form" stage plays and paintings distorted nature into such disturbing answers to reality? How is it that his portraits, elongating or compressing his models' facial features into haunted visages swimming in psychedelic whorls of color, seem to stare out at the viewer through liquid eyes—as if the canvas were some membrane between our own rational world and some other multidimensional universe? And why is it that there are certain performance events in our lives, perhaps like those practiced by Witkiewicz, that can strike us so profoundly, and yet defy our ability to rationally talk about them afterward, lacking as we do the language to express the movement of thought we experienced?

I was an American high-schooler in Zakopane, Poland, once home to Witkacy[1] during the years he formulated his theories and aesthetics. I

---

1. Witkacy, the name he gave himself as an artist, combines fragments of S.I. Witkiewicz's last and first names. I will use his preferred name in the remainder of the essay.

was the same age Witkacy had been when he had written his first philosophical treatises on dualism, Schopenhauer, and the metaphysics of
dreams. I was no such scholar, however. This summer night, I was a
tourist, like millions of others that have visited Zakopane (due in part to
the work of Witkacy's father, the elder Witkiewicz, who had cam-
paigned for an active tourist industry with his landscapes of the Tatra
Mountains). I had been invited to see a play I had never heard of called
The Madman and the Nun. What was to follow completely turned my
small conception of theatre upside-down.

Upon entering the theatre space, my fellow spectators and I were met
with a labyrinth of incense-clogged rooms we needed to pass through
in order to reach the auditorium where the play would begin. In this
liminal zone, though, the performance had already begun. On one plat-
form suspended over the corridor, a woman dressed as a nun wracked
in throngs of ecstasy moaned a mantra and lazily swung a smoking
censer. As we negotiated the narrow passageways and ducked under
misshapen doorframes, we heard from other rooms the muffled echoes
of insane shrieks and sobs. Once we reached the auditorium, the drama
that proceeded offered no comforting link back to reality. In the course
of the play, the madman in the title hung himself, died, and, in the next
act—while his corpse was still on stage—entered again. Accompanying
him was his doctor/warden, who had also died in the previous act.

I left the theatre in a dazzled state. Part of me never returned from that
place, and the psychological experience I had there is neither repeatable,
nor accessible by my own memory to this day. The lapse of that moment
in my consciousness was only addling at first; as a high-schooler I didn't
give it much thought. But in the years following I have grown more upset
at the loss, indignant that a function so personal and intimate as my
memory could be so unreliable. I concluded that something precious had
been robbed from me by the very nature of the event itself.

Since then, I have attempted to recover that moment of profound
metaphysical experience by outside means. I revisited the journal I

had kept that summer. The entry for that night consists of one small paragraph, lacking any but the most general and vague descriptions of the performance. The only words amounting to any significance are the title of the piece, the date (I believed it had been written in the 1920s), and that the author (I hadn't bothered to record the name) had committed suicide in 1939.

Several years later, I rediscovered Witkacy while wandering through the stacks of my college library in Minnesota. I noticed an anthology entitled *The Madman and the Nun and Other Plays.* I almost stole it from the shelf! Fancying that I could somehow recover at least a piece of the experience of Pure Form, I read all I could, plumbing the archives of several libraries.

Witkacy called for a new type of play, which would allow the audience to experience a metaphysical feeling, "i.e. the experience of the mystery of existence as unity in plurality" through a work which did not consist of a "reproduction of the visible world or real feelings, but a purely formal unity which ties the given elements into an indissoluble whole."[2]

To a normal, realistic mind, this new type of play appears ridiculous. Three characters dressed in red enter, "a kindly old man enters leading a cat on a string," a glass of water falls, and they all weep, the man shoots a little girl who has just crawled in from the left, and the men in red sing and dance, etc.

Witkacy's painting was no more comprehensible to sane members of society. The 1920s saw the operation of the S.I. Witkiewicz Portrait Painting Firm, which had the motto: "The customer must be satisfied. Misunderstandings are unimaginable." Strict rules of the firm were listed as to where and when the sittings would take place and exactly

---

2. Stanislaw Ignacy Witkiewicz, "Introduction to the Theory of Pure Form in the Theatre," *Avant-Garde Drama: Major Plays and Documents Post World War I*, eds. Bernard F. Dukore and Daniel C. Gerould (New York: Bantam, 1969), 489.

how the interaction between artist and client was to be conducted.[3] Witkacy experimented with nicotine, alcohol, cocaine, peyote, morphine and ether. The various combinations and amounts of these narcotics are listed at the bottoms of the portraits. Prominent citizens and acquaintances of Witkacy could commission portraits of themselves from the artist, with the amount and type of drug to be selected by the patron. *The Rules of the S.I. Witkiewicz Portrait Painting Firm* listed the various types of portraits as C, C & Co, Et, C & H, C & CO & Et, etc.

Pure Form, if one were to impose a nutshell summary upon it, was a movement to reject the confines of mimesis. Rather than imitating reality, it was the answer *to* reality.[4] As Witkacy dictated, in its ideal form, Pure Form was to be the manifestation of a metaphysical feeling experienced on the part of the artist and passed through the entire work. This metaphysical feeling should be felt by the audience members as well, so

---

3 Daniel Gerould, "Introduction," *The Madman and the Nun and Other Plays*, translated & edited by Daniel C. Gerould and C. S. Durer, with a foreword by Jan Kott (Seattle, University of Washington Press, 1968), xl.

4 Pure Form may also be understood in context of the mainstream and *avant garde* modes of theatre which preceded it. Pure Form abandons nineteenth-century theatre—realism and naturalism. Anti-naturalistic, anti-psychological, and anti-symbolistic, Witkacy's theater dispenses with consistency in plot and predictability in psychological characters. Plot, cause, and effect should be substituted with a configuration of events that are loosely related and governed by the internal formal logic of the play and not by outside conventions. In this way, Pure Form escapes the sin of *lying,* which pollutes mimetic theatre. "In the theatre of Pure Form," writes Janusz Degler, "there is no lie, since nothing is imitated or pretended. This theatre is just a means of expressing 'the artistic truth' exclusively." Janusz Degler, "Witkacy's Theory of Theatre," *Russian Literature* 22.2 (Aug 1987): 144. The point is to have a play where the audience finds itself in a world of formal beauty, which has a truth of its own and a logic of its own. See also Daniel Gerould, *Witkacy: Stanislaw Ignacy Witkiewicz as an Imaginative Writer* (Seattle: U of Washington P, 1981); Wladimir Krysinski, "The Pragmatics of Dialogue in the Theatre of S.I. Witkiewicz," *Modern Drama* 27.1 (March 1984); and Lech Sokol, "The Metaphysics of Sex: Strindberg, Weininger and S.I. Witkiewicz," *Theatre Research International* 12.1 (Spring 1987).

that they leave the theatre as if having "just awakened from some strange dream, in which even the most ordinary things had a strange, unfathomable charm, characteristic of dream reveries, and unlike anything else in the world."[5] In this way, the audience is introduced to an experiential dimension that allows them to revise their self-perceptions and that of the surrounding world.

What I had seen as a youth in Zakopane was most likely *not* Pure Form, if Witkacy were to have been there to judge. He had, himself, despaired early on at the thought whether achieving Pure Form on stage was even possible. In his 1920 *Introduction to the Theory of Pure Form in the Theatre*, he wrote that it would be easier to expound upon his ideas if he could use examples from current theatre of Pure Form to illustrate his points, but "for the time being there are no such works, and, as we ourselves admit, it is even doubtful that there will be."[6] Certainly the company that performed *The Madman and the Nun* for me and my theatre companions in Zakopane were removed from the possibility of Pure Form by their very humanity—a fact Witkacy could not overlook.

For Witkacy, humans were not part of the metaphysical world, and ultimately only served to contaminate it. Ideally, Pure Form would be able to avoid the use of humans, but for Witkacy, this was not a possibility. Indeed, as an artist, he tried to avoid contact with his human subjects as much as possible.[7]

5. Stanislaw Ignacy Witkiewicz, "On a New Type of Play," *Dramatic Theory and Criticism: Greeks to Grotowski*, ed. Bernard F. Dukore (Fort Worth: Harcourt, 1974), 977.

6 Witkacy, "Introduction to the Theory of Pure Form in the Theatre," 491.

7 Paragraph 3 of the rules of the *S.I. Witkiewicz Painting Firm* laid down the law of how human contact was to proceed.
"Any kind of criticism on the part of the customer is *absolutely* ruled out. The customer may not like the portrait, but the Firm cannot permit even the slightest comment without a special dispensation. If the Firm had allowed itself the luxury of listening to the customers' views, it would have gone out if its mind a long time ago. WE PUT PARTICULAR STRESS ON THIS PARAGRAPH, SINCE IT IS EXTREMELY

As a playwright, Witkacy made explicit references to the divisions between the human and the metaphysical characters. In *The Water Hen*, Alice, the duchess of Nevermore, is a being from the normal world; she is governed simply by hunger and desire to possess. "You're just a phantom. An imagined value," she tells Elizabeth. Arguing that the Water Hen never had a hold on her late husband, she goes on to claim, "I'm not at all jealous of you. I prefer reality to your spiritual seductions in the fourth dimension." Alice is much more comfortable with the daily world where the conscious, rational mind governs the perception of reality. She is out of her element in the dream world and thus chooses to dismiss it; she assumes that what she doesn't know cannot hurt her. *The metaphysical realm is accessible, however, and quite real.* It is populated in Witkacy's works by artists, madmen and criminals. In *The Crazy Locomotive*, two criminals disguised as locomotive engineers hijack a passenger train and pilot it at breakneck speed towards their inevitable destruction in order to rise above the monotony and banality of the three-dimensional world. In *The Water Hen*, Richard de Kordowa-Korbowski, yet another criminal in disguise, tells Alice he has loved her only, "even in the thick of crimes so monstrous as to be four-dimensional and non-Euclidean in their swinishness."

Since humans were the main part of the theatre, Pure Form could never quite be achieved. Perhaps Julia's line at the end of *The Crazy*

DIFFICULT TO RESTRAIN THE CUSTOMER FROM MAKING COMMENTS WHICH ARE REALLY QUITE UNCALLED FOR…The Firm's nerves must be respected, considering how extremely difficult its job is." Qtd. in Gerould, "Introduction," xl. These rules kept the profane models at a distance, in order to allow him to capture their metaphysical essence on his canvasses. Other perceived eccentric behavior dictated the precise structure Witkacy imposed over his dealings with humanity. His door posted the hours during which he would receive different people, depending on whether they were his friends or tradesmen. From 3:30 to 4:00 a.m. he would see his tailor and from 4:00 to 4:30 a.m. he would see his butcher (though Gerould points out that apparently no one paid attention to these rules, least of all Witkacy).

Locomotive, voices Witkacy's own frustration with all-too-human actors. Confounded by the arrival of the would-be-hero Valery Bean, just when things are starting to get interesting (the train is hurtling toward a head-on collision), she cries, "Nothing beautiful can exist in this world! The human animal always interferes and spoils everything!"[8] While Pure Form consisted of the synthesis of all the elements, humans were the variables that could not be controlled by the artist, as could the strokes of the paint brush or the notes on a musical score.

It wasn't enough for me to read about Witkacy's theory, however. I needed to practice it. When a spot opened up one season in the student theatre group on campus, I jumped at the chance to direct a Pure Form play, Witkacy's *The Crazy Locomotive.* The enterprise was a frustrating one. I experienced what I (perhaps pretentiously) imagined to be Witkacy's frustration at trying to manipulate human actors so that they would conform to a pure and synthesized composition.

The actors needed to conform to a strict performance theory in order to hope to contribute to Pure Form. They were to act not according to any Stanislavskian technique in which they would experience the characters' emotions. Nor should they engage in impersonation. Instead, they were to function as part of the whole synthesis of the piece, much like the color red would function in a painting.

The young actors, however, were too intent on acting according to the ingrained standards of nineteenth-century realism. They balked at my directorial decisions, wondering whether they would be *accessible* to the audience. In the more extreme cases, they accused the project of serving only masturbatory ends, paying no attention to the needs and expectations of the paying audience. On my own part, my humanity got in the way as well, as I tried to force the text to speak with a present

---

8 Witkacy, "The Crazy Locomotive," *The Madman and the Nun and the Crazy Locomotive: Three Plays (Including the Water Hen) by Stanislaw Ignacy Witkiewicz,* eds. Daniel Gerould and C.S. Durer (New York: Applause, 1989), 103

language of intelligibility. Looking back on what I now consider a very poor choice, I hoped to have made an allegorical allusion to the anxiety of the age of communication and rapid obsolescence of the state of the art by using Witkacy's play about the anxiety of mechanization and the critique of Futurism.

An experience on a summer trip to Cape Cod plunged me more directly into Witkacy's metaphysical dimension. Launched from the dock of Provincetown harbor, my wife and I set forth on a "scientific" whale-watching vessel as part of an enterprise which capitalizes on taking tourists to the spots where whales surface and play. On a successful day, whales in numbers of thirty or more float close to the surface and splash their extremities—or, in the *coup de grace* of the touristic experience, breech the surface. In these cases, the whale will shoot up perpendicularly, the majority of its bulk rising into the air, and then crash back into the sea again in a wonderfully climactic display of power and water. Such sights were rare to see, but commonly hinted at as distinct possibilities by the crew to excite the passengers on our outbound voyage.

As the boat tooled out in search of the whales, we waited impatiently, eventually losing sight of Provincetown and losing ourselves in the vast emptiness of Nantucket Sound. Suddenly, the tourists leapt into excited motion as they found themselves surrounded with whales appearing out of nowhere. Splashing, breaching, and lazily drifting past the boat, the whales seemed to be studying us even as we gazed voyeuristically into their private life. The boat had come to a halt in order to get a good long look at the display, but when it was time to head back, the guide informed us that we would need to wait. Sonar had indicated that a humpback whale was directly beneath the craft, and the crew hesitated to start engines for fear that the propeller would hurt the whale.

As I leaned over the railing, waiting for the animal to join its companions so we could return to the port, I watched the surface of the water lapping up against the side of the boat. Slowly, the green of the water mottled into a darker shadow and then resolved itself into a giant shape just beneath the surface.

I could see the whale, in all of its strangeness—a being from another world entirely—as it glided slowly beneath the thin surface of the water that separated our two worlds. An eye fixed on me. Its world was by far bigger and deeper than mine (the area of the world ocean two thirds the size of dry land) and completely unknown to me, despite the fact that our worlds occupied the same planet. The encounter turned my stomach. The meeting of the two worlds seemed uncanny, or at least not meant for my eyes—or the whale's for that matter. Brought into such close contact, the denizens of each world would have threatened to drive one another insane had it not been for the filter of reason that had been clamped down on my mind in school, striating my consciousness into that which could be explained by scientific categorization. Who knows what structures—if any—the whale used to protect itself?

Alfred Jarry's pataphysics dictates that the space we inhabit may be understood as the surface that exists between the world of three dimensions and the other, unknown world. In *Caesar Antichrist* (1896), the *entr'acte* between Acts II and III consists of the simple stage direction, "The whales appear at the surface of the sea."[9] In context of the narrative of *Caesar Antichrist*, the surfacing begins to erase the horizon that separates the positive and negative world. Consequently, the presence of the Christ and Antichrist, respectively, may pass through the tenuous membrane, forcing the unknown into the known world, and *vice versa*. The coming to the surface of whales is a grand signifier of the meeting of the two worlds. The tension between the two worlds is much like that in the embrace of two soap bubbles, the one bubble familiar to us and the other a multidimensional space ungraspable by our limited faculties.

The only way to begin to comprehend the unknown, for Jarry, Witkacy, and others, is to tease out the tension in the membrane that

---

9 Alfred Jarry, *Caesar Antichrist*, trans. James Bierman (Tucson: Omen Press, 1971).

separates it from the known world. The rational mind, in this case, imposes a border of reason over the unknown and the unconscious, and all that cannot be categorized and explained by sound, rational thought. By virtue of this border, the unknown becomes invisible to the rational spectator.[10]

Daniel Gerould writes at length about the blurring between the borders of physical and metaphysical in the Pure Form plays of Witkacy:

> For a few moments it becomes possible to see around the contradictions inherent in reality and perceive both the thing and its opposite at the same time. These movements of metaphysical revelation, portrayed as though a curtain were being drawn or a secret panel opening within the mind—disclose a new dimension in which we are outside the forms of time and space, viewing both sides of a duality concurrently...[11]

Witkacy's stage becomes the surface between the conscious and unconscious. This is the world that to a normal eye would appear as absurd as Trefaldi's rantings in Witkacy's *The Crazy Locomotive* (1923). When heard from the ground as he speeds past on his frantic locomotive, Trefaldi is nothing but a mad hijacker. On the train itself, however, a space which transcends the mundane reality of the earth's surface, the masks are stripped away and the truth is revealed—a synthesis of sound and matter and gesture and form and color. In this world it is not ridiculous for a character that died in the first act to return in the second,

---

10 As Breton's *Surrealist Manifesto* explained, the primordial area of the dreams is censored with rational thought. The only way we are able to access the world of dreams, argued Breton, is when they somehow interrupt and interfere with rational thought. Andre Breton, "The First Surrealist Manifesto," *Surrealism*, trans. Patrick Waldberg (New York: McGraw-Hill, 1971).

11 Gerould, 1981, 168-169.

despite the fact that the corpse is still plainly visible on stage. Nor does the non-realistic, non-developmental dialogue seem forced, absurd or ridiculous. Instead, this world can be seen as a sublime combination that creates a purely formal piece.[12] It is not a mirror of life, but a horizon in which the beings of another world emerge to occupy the space and manipulate the surface tension, however briefly.

No matter how bizarre, the events in a Pure Form drama do not transpire to surprise and shock us (as did the dada plays, devoid of any governance dictating which event would follow the previous one); the goal is not to alienate the audience or start them out of a hypnotic state imposed upon them by the stagnant art of the day. Witkacy desires the opposite effect: The mind of the spectator must be fully in accordance with what happens on the stage—just as, to paraphrase Andre Breton in *The First Surrealist Manifesto*, the dreaming mind is fully satisfied with what happens to it.

Unity with the audience is possible because the fourth dimension is not a new territory but rather one that used to be regularly accessed by the ancients. Witkacy saw the whole tradition of theatre as a decline, starting the moment the Greeks began to secularize their religious rituals. Through his Pure Form works, he attempted to recapture what was lost at that moment by assuming a primordial state of art and theatre in which metaphysical and physical were one and the same. Up to the moment of loss, primordial culture enjoyed time in which performance on stage was identical with myth. Witkacy wrote:

---

12 Like the backdrop of Chekhov's *The Seagull*, in which the lake, viewed at sunset is the backdrop of Konstantin Treplev's strange symbolic experimental work, Act I of *The Water Hen* consists of the horizon meeting the edge of the sea, delineating the boundary of two separate worlds. In Act III, the curtain is opened to reveal the same backdrop as in Act I; the temporal and spatial worlds collapse into a total surface.

> In the times of Greece it was not the content which was
> important. Everybody knew it, due to the fact that
> everybody knew the myths. It was the very process of
> becoming and rising of things which, similarly to what
> occurs in music, endowed the experiences of the specta-
> tors with a new dimension. This process had a power of
> carrying the spectators into another world, into the
> world of metaphysical experience, far from any com-
> monplace reality.[13]

This type of theatre did not last long, according to Witkacy's
chronology. The changing social conditions brought a gradual trivial-
ization of religion. The rituals lost their meaning and became simply
automatic. Concurrently, the gods became more trivialized and began
to resemble men. Witkacy links the slow process of decline in art to the
shift from art's metaphysical goal to a mimetic one. "It started to consider the imitation of everyday life, commonplace relations and situa-
tions as its main task. In this way it destroyed the border line which
previously used to separate art from life and it slowly began to be
equaled with life itself."[14] Only with the complete abandonment of
mimesis, then, could the pure art of theatre, lost to countless genera-
tions, be recovered. In its current state, during the time Witkacy was
writing, Pure Form asks whether it is possible to return to this mode in
which the metaphysical and physical are again unified so that the audience would be able to experience metaphysical feelings in the way the
ancients experienced them.

Finally, let me remark that Pure Form has nothing to do with spiritu-
ality. Pure Form is a radical surfacing of two dimensions (metaphysical
and physical) into one world; it is not an invocation, evocation, transfer,

---

13 Quoted in Degler, 151.
14 Quoted in Degler, 152.

or transformation of one world to another; it cannot be invited with the lighting of incense, chanting or other trappings of romantic ritualistic communal theatre. *The metaphysical is already there, but not readily accessible to the viewer, who has been separated from it in a gradual process of decline beginning with the introduction of mimesis into art.* Pure Form nurses the spectator into the state in which he or she would be able to receive the metaphysical feeling being radiated by the synthesis of the forms on stage, the unity of multiplicities, just as they would act as receptors for the concentric beams of green light emanating from the lamp post in *The Water Hen.*

Cortázar and Pataphysics

M. Alejandro Riberi
Translated by Mark Singer[1]

I have it on the best authority. *Omnis a Deo scientia,* which means: *Omnis,* all; *a Deo,* wisdom; *scientia,* comes from God. Which explains the whole miraculous revelation.

—Alfred Jarry, *Ubu Roi*[2]

The Exploits and Opinions of Doctor Faustroll, Pataphysician by Alfred Jarry constitutes without any doubt the "bible" of all good pataphysicians. However, as a bible, the explicit content of the doctrine is fairly reduced [*réduit*]. In spite of this paucity of information, we attempt herein to show the origins of pataphysical thought and its treatment in the work of Cortázar.

Faustroll is above all else a book produced out of the anti-positivist reaction. Jarry records [*y consigne*] a large critique of fundamental scientific knowledge at an historical moment when the sciences, in particular physio-mathematics, enjoyed an absolute prestige.

---

1 This text was written by the author in Spanish and then rewritten (also by the author) in French. I have further translated the latter into English. [Trans.]

2 Alfred Jarry, *The Ubu Plays,* ed. Simon Watson Taylor, trans. Cyril Connolly and Simon Watson Taylor (New York: Grove Press, 1969), 67.

The arguments included in *Faustroll* can be synthesized [synthétisés] as follows:

Science, to construct its model of reality, selects, sometimes for extra-scientific reasons, the facts of the totality of phenomena which constitute the universe. To the events that are unique, particular, it (science) attributes a status of general phenomena.

Science bases itself on the supposition that if an observed phenomenon takes place under the same conditions a sufficient number of times, it is therefore possible to induce that this phenomenon will always occur in the same manner and to establish a general "law."

But the principle of induction, according to Jarry, is nothing else but a simple "prejudice of universal belief [consentement]" that he rejects in keeping with his aristocratic disdain for such "democratic" notions:

> Contemporary science is founded upon the principle of induction: most people have seen a certain phenomenon precede or follow some other phenomenon most often, and conclude therefrom that it will ever be thus. Apart from other considerations, this is true only in the majority of cases, depends upon the point of view, and is codified only for convenience—if that![3]

> Universal assent is already a quite miraculous and incomprehensible prejudice.[4]

What then are the principles of pataphysics that would replace the deficiencies of "Science"? The classical definition is found in Book II of *Faustroll*, "Elements of Pataphysics," in the chapter entitled, "Definition."

---

3 Alfred Jarry, *Exploits and Opinions of Doctor Faustroll, Pataphysician,* trans. Simon Watson Taylor (Boston: Exact Change, 1996), 22.
4 Ibid, 23.

Pataphysics will examine the laws governing exceptions, and will explain the universe supplementary to this one; or, less ambitiously, will describe a universe which can be—and perhaps should be—envisaged in the place of the traditional one, since the laws that are supposed to have been discovered in the traditional universe are also correlations of exceptions, albeit more frequent ones, but in any case accidental data which, reduced to the status of unexceptional exceptions, possess no longer even the virtue of originality.[5]

It is Jarry who had the insight [*l'intuition*] that, despite the progress of scientific knowledge, the question of existence remained unanswered. Moreover, not only had science no answer to the problem of the ultimate ends of the universe (and thus it would seem that, in offering no answer, traditional religious explanations were relegated to the domain of myth pure and simple), but furthermore science was incapable of establishing the necessity of any phenomenon and of existence itself, [a problem] which has preoccupied existential philosophy from Heidegger to Sartre. Jarry seems to have realized that the simple fact of a given event being either habitually preceded or succeeded by another given event offers no guarantee that the same two events invariably and necessarily occur together. For practical reasons, of course, we can conclude that certain events will be linked, following a pre-established law, but the absence of necessity, on a purely philosophical plane, subsists.

In the works of Cortázar, pataphysical perceptions and humor tend to confirm the exceptionality of Aristotelian logic and Euclidean laws. His narration involves the spontaneous examination of all that is offered as dogma, received wisdom [*Grande Habitude*], or hegemonic knowledge.

---

5 Ibid, 21-22.

As in Jarry, humor in Cortázar serves to provoke disdain in the face of the quotidian and therefore, implicitly, signals the existence of a second version of things, a reading of reality distinct from stereotypical readings of previously agreed upon logical categories. Cortázar has a large register of humor that always puts the reader on alert. Humor also serves to introduce elements of *costumbrismo porteño* in several episodes on "this side of" *Rayuela*.[6]

For Cortázar, in the exceptional is born the possibility of rescuing the object of plannification [*l'applanissement*] from scientific reduction and pragmatic usage. Thus, in the short story, "Las Babas del Diablo," after having established the analogy between photographer and raconteur, Cortázar postulates that the precise action of the first capture of an object reveals that thing in its unique essence, in its exceptionality. In the same manner, in "Las Armas Secretas," he denounces the tendency to compare experiences and objects, to convert them into something general and anonymous:

> It is odd, the folks who think they are making a bed are always making a bed; for them extending their hand is always extending their hand; for them opening a tin of sardines is unaccountably [*indéfiniment*] opening the same tin of sardines. 'But if everything is exceptional'…[7]

---

6 Cortázar knew and had ties to several humorists who in the 1950s participated in different reviews published in Buenos Aires. These publications, which combined political satire and parodies of quotidian life, also included the pataphysical "doctrine" introduced in Argentina principally by Esteban Fassio, a friend of Cortázar, who wrote in a revue *"Letra y Línea."* Other Argentinian humorists like Caésar Bruto (Carlos Warnes), author of a long text, a sort of second epigraph, that can be found at the beginning of Cortázar's *Marelle*, and Landró (Juan Carlos Colombres) y Copi (Raúl Damonte Taborda) have the same orientation.

7 Julio Cortázar, *Las armas secretas* (Buenos Aires: Edit. Sudamericana, 1972), 114.

What Cortázar calls a "notion" or "sentiment" of the fantastic in his short stories is always something that surges in the quotidian and that is at the same time the quotidian. It is by way of apprehending this singularity, forbidden by our own mental habits, that we arrive at the "notion." In this regard, the fantastic is not an evasion of reality, but on the contrary, a genre [*forme*] different from the formulation of abstract, logical categories.

But the fantastic is inextricable from pataphysics; it is an order less communicable, an order of exceptions where scientific explanations fail. Capturing one's exceptionality and transforming it to an axis of narration opens another vision of reality.

We can say that Cortázar utilizes a technique that permits the extraction of objects from their habitual context and places them, sometimes incongruously, on another plane and, by way of this new perspective, pierces their occult essence. By imitating, with absurdist humor, one can pretend to destroy the limits of reality and erase the inhibiting conditions of quotidian existence. This humor is designed to overwhelm the reader by signaling the uselessness of the bourgeois canons he lives amongst, pushing him [the reader] toward a search [à la recherché] for an alternative that can transform the ordinary into the extraordinary and the exceptional. In their absolute quest, the surrealists attempted every method to abolish the realist concept of life. Among these remedies [recours], one finds humor and mockery. In surrealism, art occupies an important part of life and receives the same treatment. Even if the method of this recourse can appear to be frivolous, the objective of the quest is not. At this level, we find in *Rayuela* the same way of posing the problem. The quest for the *marvelous,* that in *Rayuela* has diverse names such as *Kibboutz,* center, mandala, etc., seems to borrow from the same paths.

The Cortazarian idea of constructing fictions on principles other than those of the causality that determine the psychology of the characters is also eminently pataphysical. This notion appears in a programmatic form in the famous chapter of *Marelle*. Here Morelli establishes a text that will have an epigenous [*épigone*] unfolding for Cortázar, notoriously in his novel *62 Modelos Para Armar*.

The anarchist vision proposed by *Faustroll* is sub-adjacent in the critique of the principle of causality. Let us recall that for Jarry there exists no guarantee that events must repeat themselves as in the associations prescribed by the laws of science. Jarry's criticism of the principles of causality do not disappear in the face of the idealist arguments of Hume, whom one finds in analytical philosophy in opposition to subsequent attacks and the remissions in question. For Jarry, criticism acquires another signification: The uniformity prescribed by the principle of causality is a decoy [*leurre*] since it is but a correlation of exceptions, or fortuitous facts. Or even better: It is the proof that the exceptional can take place since, in the last instance, all phenomena are treated as purely "fortuitous" or epiphenomenal.

In *Rayeula*, the vacuity of the story in general seems to follow our postulate. The gratuitousness of what happens in the planks chapter confirms it for us:

> —Thank you. We were nailed and check-mated [*au clous et au maté*]. Why do you want nails?

> —I don't know yet, said Oliveira, confused. I went to get the box of nails and I discovered that they were all crooked. I assigned myself the task of straightening them out and it is so cold that you can guess the result...I have the impression that once I have straight nails I'll know why I have need of them.[8]

---

8 Julio Cortázar, *Rayuela* (1ra. Edición, CEP de la Biblioteca Nacional de Madrid, 1991), 196.

Cortázar, by writing, by inverting the course of events in a way that teleological ties disappear, ruptures reality. Once again, the goal is to remove us from our tridimensional world in order to take us to another "place" where the elements of reality associate differently, where our vision is directed to a point that decenters the observer and thereby opens an instance of the exceptional.

Yet pataphysics does not occupy a hegemonic place in *Rayuela*. Neither is it introduced expressly [*en tant que contenu express*]. It constitutes a perspective, a manner of seeing. Cortázar hardly mentions it in *Marelle*, thus, for example, none of the "pataphysical" conversations of Horacio and Sybille, which regularly occur in vaguely Parisian locations, are reproduced:

> We spoke of Pataphysics with the Sibylle until exhaustion,
> because it also happened to her (and this was the subject of
> our conversation as well as other obscure matters such as
> phosphorus) to ceaselessly fall upon exceptions.[9]

But it is a pataphysical gesture to include in a novel extracts of Ceferino Piriz's texts, texts that propose a geopolitical model compelled [*tire par les cheveux*] to organize the world into races and zones; and the method of organizing certain extracts found in the "serious" space of the text is also pataphysical.

The exegesis of Jarry's *Faustroll* allows the establishment of the surrealist relationship to *Rayuela* and the key to the pataphysical doctrine. "All pervading" humor, its anarchistic structure, and its quest for the exceptional and for the marvelous appear to be the most visible elements of this relationship. Pataphysics, we have said, is not an explicit subject in *Rayuela* but an attitude with which to approach [*aborder*]

---

9 Julio Cortázar, *Marelle*, traduit par Laure Guille-Bataillon et Françoise Rosset (L'imaginaire Gallimard, 1966), 14.

reality. This attitude is neither an engagement nor a rejection, but rather a combination of the two; a vision of the world and a slow traffic [*un lent commerce*], by way of humor, with the things of the world.

Jarry: Patasophe

Brian Parshall

O Zarathustra...to those who think as we do, all things themselves are dancing: they come and offer their hands and laugh and
flee-and come back. Everything goes, everything comes back; eternally rolls the wheel of being. Everything dies, everything blos-
soms again; eternally runs the year of being. Everything breaks,
everything is joined anew; eternally the same house is being built.
Everything parts, everything greets every other thing again; eternally the ring of being remains faithful to itself. In every Now,
being begins; round every Here rolls the sphere There. The center
is everywhere. Bent is the path of eternity.

—Friedrich Nietzsche,
*Thus Spoke Zarathustra: A
Book for All and None*, Third
Part (1884)[1]

The ancient metaphorical formula of the "infinite sphere whose center
is everywhere and whose circumference is nowhere" (*sphaera infinita
cuius centrum ubique circumferentia nusquaam*) is recast by Alfred Jarry
no less than three times in his writings, in at least three rather different
forms, suggesting that it held for him a particular fascination. These
occurances of the metaphor fall at critical junctures in three of his most

1. Walter Kaufmann, trans. and ed., *The Portable Nietzsche* (New York: Viking
Penguin, 1954; 1982), 329-330. The present essay is a much-condensed version of
Chapter IV of the author's dissertation; for fuller treatment, see Brian Parshall,
Tourbillon: Myth, Cosmology, Pataphysics (Santa Barbara: California Press, 2000).

important works in relation to his "science of pataphysics": *César-Antechrist* (1895), *Les Jours et les nuits* (1897), and *Gestes et opinions du Dr. Faustroll, pataphysicien* (1898; 1911).[2] Most recent discussions of the metaphor of the infinite sphere begin with a reference to Jorge Luis Borges' essay "The Fearful Sphere of Pascal," in which Borges sketches a brief history of the metaphor's employment by various writers to alternately allude to either God or the universe.[3] But as Karsten Harries has indicated, Borges' sketch is not only missing some key figures, his later suggestion that the metaphor's transference from God to the universe *followed* the astronomical discoveries of Galileo and others in the 16th century is actually *a reversal*; this "transference" both prefigured and formed the groundwork for the "new sciences."[4] Whereas Borges suggests that the shift came with Giordano Bruno, Harries states that

---

2 The first of these three texts, *César-Antechrist*, is most often translated as *Caesar-Antichrist*, despite the lack of an accent in Jarry's title. Jarry quite evidently intended the name to suggest both *before* (ante-) Christ, as well as Antichrist, but his use of the unaccented spelling is important. Despite this translation anomaly, as well as its evident dramatic form, I have never seen reference made to the 12th century *Play of Antichrist*, written during the era of Frederick Barbarossa, in any discussions of Jarry's play. See John Wright, trans. and ed., *The Play of Antichrist* (Toronto: Pontifical Institute of Medieval Studies, 1967), in which single and "third" horns sprout from a variety of heads throughout. It is *pure coincidence* that Jarry's play was published the same year as Nietzsche's *Der Antichrist* (1895); the latter had been confined to an asylum in 1889, and its publication was due largely to the efforts of his sister Elizabeth, who did so much to distort his thought and his work's reception.

3 D.A. Yates and J.E. Irby, eds., *Labyrinths* (NY: New Directions, 1964), 189-192. Borges' essay begins and ends with nearly identical sentences, in which he suggests that universal history may be "the history of the different intonations given a handful of metaphors." This essay is cited in the notes to Anthony Melville's translation, introduced and annotated by Alastair Brotchie, *Caesar Antichrist* (London: Atlas Press, 1992), 42. Brotchie states that Borges "omits the one example of this definition of God that Jarry would certainly have been familiar with, in Rabelais (Bk. III, ch. 13)." While this is true, Borges does cite another example in Rabelais, though he does not give the writer's name ["the last chapter of the last book of *Pantagruel*"(190)]. There is a slight difference here, however; the latter example contains only the word "intellectual," whereas that cited by Brotchie reads "infinite and intellectual."

4 Harries, "The Infinite Sphere: Comments on the History of a Metaphor," *Journal of the History of Philosophy* 13 (1975): 5-15. I will suggest near the end of this essay that Jarry had rather different ideas in regard to this "transference."

"Bruno was here following the fifteenth century cardinal Nicolas Cusanus."[5] Jarry was surely aware of Cusanus (Nicholas of Cusa) although he does not seem to mention him anywhere in his work; he most certainly encountered his name in the writings of François Rabelais, who mentions him twice in passing.[6]

In the same chapter in which Rabelais first alludes to Cusanus, he also makes his first mention of ancient Greek philosopher-poet Empedocles, whom he again addresses only twice in passing.[7] Jarry's poem "Empédocle" was written in March of 1888 (he was fourteen years old) and was among the papers from his childhood writings that he later collected under the title "Ontogénie" ("Ontogenesis," or

---

5 Harries sees Cusanus' notion of "transference" as inherent *in the metaphor itself.*

6 Second Book, Chapter 14, "How Panurge related the manner how he escaped out of the hands of the Turks," first paragraph: "...and so Cusanus will be deceived in his conjecture. Remember that I have told you of it, and given you fair advertisement in time and place convenient." See also Fifth Book, Chapter 25, "How the thirty-two persons at the ball fought" (in other words, a game of chess, anticipating Lewis Carroll by some 300+ years): "Seeing them then turn about on one foot after they had made their honours, we compared them to your tops or gigs, such as boys use to whip about, making them turn round so swiftly that they sleep, as they call it, and motion cannot be perceived, but resembles rest, its contrary; so that if you make a point or mark on some part of one of those gigs, 'twill be perceived not as a point, but a continual line, in a most divine manner, as Cusanus has wisely observed." Trans. Sir Thomas Urquhart of Cromarty and Peter Antony Motteux.

7 Pantagruel: "O companion! if I could mount up as well as I can swallow down, I would long ago have been above the sphere of the moon with Empedocles. But I cannot tell what the devil this means." See also Third Book, Chapter 16, "How Pantagruel adviseth Panurge to consult with the Sibyl of Panzoust," in which he says of the latter, "Therefore in my conceit it is not an improper kind of speech to call them sage or wise women. In confirmation of which opinion of mine, the customary style of my language alloweth them the denomination of presage women. The epithet of sage is due unto them because they are surpassing dexterous in the knowledge of most things. And I give them the title of presage, for that they divinely foresee and certainly foretell future contingencies and events of things to come. Sometimes I call them not maunettes, but monettes, from their wholesome monitions. Whether it be so, ask Pythagoras, Socrates, Empedocles, and our master Ortuinus." Jarry would later model, to some extent, his brief fragment "The Pataphysics of Sophrotatos the Armenian" [Alfred Jarry, *Œuvres Complètes*, 3 vols. (Paris: Gallimard, Bibliothèque de la Pléiade, 1972-1988), 1: 265-66] after a passage in the next chapter in Rabelais' book, Ch. 17 "How Panurge spoke to the Sibyl of Panzoust."

"coming into being; *becoming*"), inscribing on the cover that it would be "more honorable not to publish (them)."[8] There exists a fairly evident precedent, Matthew Arnold's dramatic epic poem, "Empedocles on Etna" (1852), and several authors have suggested that Arnold was influenced by German poet Friedrich Hölderlin, whose dramatic epic "Der Tod des Empedokles" was published in 1846.[9] Hölderlin, in turn, has been shown to be an important source of

---

8 See now *O.C.*, 1: 117-118. The name "Empédocle" is not, however, listed in the lengthy "Index des noms," *O.C.*, 3: 1051-1097. This is also the case with the name "Pythagore," although Jarry titles Book III, Chapter 2 of *Les Jours et les nuits* (*Days and Nights*) "Pythagoras." The name does not recur in the chapter. And yet it seems that Jarry's title can only be understood in terms of the "before Christ" meaning of *César-Antechrist*. Here one must recognize that for Pythagoras, number was everything, and everything number. The only numbers that appear in the chapter are "quarante-trois…C'est bien cela, quarante degrés et trois dixièmes." These numbers relate exactly to a passage in the Bible, Isaiah 40:3, the so-called "Messianic prophesy": "Every valley shall be exalted, and every mountain and hill shall be made low: and the crooked shall be made straight, and the rough places plain." See here Robin Small, "Zarathustra's Gateway," *History of Philosophy Quarterly* 15.1 (January 1998) 97 n 22. The passage from Isaiah relates to the metaphor of the infinite sphere in that it suggests a "smoothing of the orb" in an attempt to level mountains and raise valleys in order to render the earth a "harmonious sphere" for the "return of (or to) God." The Book of Isaiah has been dated to the 6th century BCE, when Confucius, the Buddha, Zoroaster (Old Iranian *Zarathustra*), Isaiah, and Pythagoras were alive contemporaneously; here we have an indication of what Jarry was attempting with his "Antechrist": a synthesis of some (or all) of these ancient figures. See also J.A. Philip, *Pythagoras and Early Pythagoreanism* (Toronto: U of Toronto P, 1968): Chapter 6, "Pythagorean number theory," which begins "The number theory of the Pythagoreans derives from their cosmology and, in its principal aspects, *is* cosmology."

9 See Fred L. Burwick, "Hölderlin and Arnold: Empedocles on Etna," *Comparative Literature* 17 (1965) 24-42. Both of these dramatic poems have complicated publishing histories; both were revised several times, and held back from publication at least once. Jarry's poem, perhaps surprisingly, is not in dramatic form. Edgar Allan Poe, in his cosmological prose poem *Eureka* (1848), translated by Baudelaire in 1864, alludes to Empedocles in his opening paragraph, and throughout to his cosmology, but never mentions his name. Baudelaire's translation of Poe is the first ("alphabetically") of Dr. Faustroll's *livres pairs*, the books that he takes with him on his voyage "From Paris to Paris by Sea." *O.C.*, 1: 661.

Nietzsche's great enthusiasm for Empedocles.[10] The origins of the metaphor of the infinite sphere have been traced to Empedocles through the writings of thirteenth century encyclopaedist Vincent de Beauvais, although it can no longer be found in the fragmentary remains of his poetry.[11] Jarry mentions Vincent only once in his writings, and only in passing, in the essay "La Vierge et l'Enfant," published in the April 1895 issue of his print journal *L'Ymagier*, a few months before the publication of *César-Antechrist*.[12]

Jarry's earliest recasting of the metaphor of the infinite sphere is in his essay "Visions actuelles et future," published in *L'Art littéraire* in May 1894; it is later incorporated into the "Heraldic Act" (sc. vi) of *César-Antechrist*.[13] Here, in a section entitled "Du bâton-à-physique,"

10 Walter Kaufmann, *Nietzsche: Philosopher, Psychologist, Antichrist* (Princeton: Princeton UP, 1974) 306 n. See also Raymond Furness, "Nietzsche and Empedocles," *Journal of the British Society for Phenomenology* (2 May 1971): 91-94. Empedocles: "Stepping from summit to summit, not to travel only one path of words to the end." (Diels' *fragment* 24, as translated by John Burnett). Nietzsche: "In the mountains the shortest way is from peak to peak, but for that one must have long legs." (*Thus Spoke Zarathustra*, First Part, "On Reading and Writing"). Jarry: "A giant only counts by Himalayas." ("Livres d'Étrennes: 'Le Calendrier du Facteur,'" ("New Year's Gift Books: 'The Postman's Calendar,'") *La Plume* 15 January 1903; *O.C.*, 2: 397.

11 See Robin Small, "Nietzsche and a Platonist Tradition of the Cosmos: Center Everywhere and Circumference Nowhere," *Journal of the History of Ideas* 44 (1983): 89-104, who provides the relevant citations, 91 and notes. Small also provides several uses of the metaphor by writers omitted by both Borges and Harries. Jarry has left several "fragments" of text, some *explicitly* entitled as such; see Chapters 39 and 40 of *Faustroll*; the "writings" of Marcel Duchamp exist almost exclusively as fragments.

12 His name is included in the "Index des noms" to the Pléiade in Jarry's *Œuvres Complètes*, but here he is given as "Nicolas-Dauphin de, appelé par Jarry: Vincent de; 1668?-1753?; graveur français." This is because Jarry only mentions Vincent (c.1190-1264) here in his print journal, in the context of some of the woodcuts he is republishing. But it is somewhat astonishing that the editors did not know his identity; his *Speculum majus* ("Great Mirror") was probably the most important European encyclopaedia up to the eighteenth-century.

13 *O.C.*, 1: 337-341; 289-290.

following a brief allusion to the leaping *bâton* of Chant III, strophe v of Lautréamont's *Les Chants de Maldoror* (1869)[14] Jarry writes: "You are a wheel whose substance alone exists, the diameter of the circle without circumference creating a plane by its rotation around its median point. The substance of your diameter is a Point."[15] Now one may immediately object that there is no "sphere" mentioned here, but it seems fairly clear that "the circle without circumference" and "the substance of your diameter is a Point" are allusions to the ancient metaphor. Falling as it does in the "Heraldic Act" of *César-Antechrist*, and with the origins of heraldry in Europe dating to the 12th century, Jarry may be referring to certain linguistic peculiarities in the description of spherical and circular objects in the era that also saw the origins of modern European poetry. It has been noted that "the Old French language possesses no single unambiguous word to express the notion of sphericity...the term 'round' was applied to both circles and spheres."[16]

Although I have found no direct allusions to the metaphor of the infinite sphere in *Ubu Roi*, there are indirect allusions in some related texts: Jarry tells his audience in his preliminary address that the action of the play "takes place in Poland, that is to say Nowhere," and in his written program further remarks that this country is "so legendary, so dismembered

---

14 See *O.C.*, 1: xix and note; also 1133, 289 n. 1; as well as 1140, 339 n. *Maldoror* is the thirteenth of Dr. Faustroll's *livres pairs*.

15 "Tu es une roue dont la substance seule subsiste, le diamètre du cercle sans circonférence créant un plan par sa rotation autour de son point médian. La substance de ton diamètre est un Point."

16 Jill Tattersall, "Sphere or Disk? Allusions to the Shape of the Earth in Some Twelfth-Century and Thirteenth-Century Vernacular French Works," *Modern Language Review*, 76.1 (January 1981): 31-46; this quote 34-35. Meaning was determined by context and the use of visual imagery, such as "rond comme une pomme," but while very clear in some contexts, it remains unclear in others. A few lines later, Jarry writes parenthetically: "—laissons le disque quelques siècles encore aux accessoires et à l'homme..." ("let us leave the disk for a few more centuries to the unessentials and to man...").

that it is well-qualified to be this particular Nowhere, or, in terms of a putative Franco-Greek etymology, a distantly interrogative somewhere."[17] While Poland certainly continued to exist in the imagination of the Poles, as Jarry would surely agree, and in the imagination of anyone who had ever known the word "Poland," at that time Poland had *lost its periphery*.[18] While "periphery" and "circumference" are often used interchangeably, the difference is largely in relation to the form being circumscribed; the latter is most often (although not always) specific to circular objects,[19] while the former is often used to describe the perimeter of an irregular shape, or an imprecise boundary, or even the area beyond a boundary. The "poles" of a polarized spherical solid are, of course, on the circumference of that sphere. Since our metaphor insists that "the circumference is nowhere," a "Pole" (a person of Polish descent), would thus have been situated

---

17 *O.C.*, 1: 401. This seems to be an allusion to the Empedoclean origins of the metaphor of the sphere. The word "pole" is of Greek origin, stemming from *polos*; the "Franco—" portion of this "putative" etymology being suggested in the French expression "*soûl comme un polonais*," or "drunk as a lord; blind drunk" (*Collins-Robert Dictionary*, s.v. "soûl"), "polonais" being French for "Polish person," or "Pole." Indeed; the idea of a "pole-land" would be of extreme interest to Jarry, particularly in regard to the *as-yet unseen* Northern and Southern poles of the Earth, as well as in regard to the Precession of the Equinoxes, related to the slow "wobble" of the Earth on its axis. See also Isaiah 24:20: "The earth shall reel to and fro like a drunkard, and shall be removed like a cottage; and the transgression thereof shall be heavy upon it; and it shall fall, and not rise again."

18 Poland was partitioned three times beginning in 1772 and ending in 1795, and remained in this "dismembered" state until 1918.

19 See the *Grand Larousse dictionnaire universel du XIXe siécle*, s.v. "circonférence." Here we are given a quote from Pascal rooted in the metaphor of the sphere, but which specifically equates God with "*un cercle dont le centre est partout et la circonférence nulle part*," omitting the word sphere as well as "*infini*." (This is the source for the title of Borges' story; in the manuscript for his *Pensées*, Pascal had replaced the crossed-out word *effroyable* with *infini*). In regard to Jarry's Ubu, however, the example given from Molière is very interesting: "Il faut un roi de théâtre qui soit gros et gras comme quatre; un roi, morbleu! qui soit entripaillé comme il faut; un roi d'une vaste circonférence, et qui puisse remplir un trône de la belle manière." It seems that Jarry must have come across this quotation (its source is not given) at a very young age.

"Nowhere." In his program notes, Jarry continues, "Nowhere is everywhere..."[20] As will be seen later, this *equation* of the equivalent terms within the ancient metaphor for "circumference" and "center" is further developed in the final chapter of *Faustroll,* where the metaphor is *mathematicized* in "modern" terms.

Jarry returns to the metaphor of the infinite sphere in his novel *Days and Nights,* Book V, Chapter 4, "Assassin's Talk" (a discussion which takes place after eating "eucharists" of hashish, this word having a similar etymology as "assassin"),[21] in which Herreb, the "German philosopher," here become "The Old Man of the Woods," says:

> I have seen a fog from hell...Oh ! I'm suffocating, oh ! how pretty it is...oh ! It holds together so well! O the center. And there, that's a molecule. The center, it's marvellous. The center, oh ! it's beautiful. Oh there ! the center. O the center of God. And its periphery. A periphery with only a center. There are gardens. O how tiring to move. I feel a peripheraesthenia...Oh there.[22]

---

20 *O.C.,* 1: 402.

21 This chapter is loaded with subtle references to the works of such earlier writers as Thomas De Quincey, Alfred de Musset, Théophile Gautier, Charles Baudelaire, and Arthur Rimbaud, of which it would be too cumbersome to treat here; suffice it to say that the eucharistic reference is to Gautier's 1846 story "Le Club des Hachichins," and the etymological link between "hashish" and "assassin," while perhaps suggested by all five writers, is perhaps most prevalent in Rimbaud's "Matinée d'ivresse" from his *Illuminations* (1886), which closes with "Voici le temps des ASSASSINS." All in all though, Jarry's chapter is structured almost exactly after Baudelaire's *Les Paradis Artificiels* (1851-1861), from the strings of puns to the visual cues.

22 *O.C.,* 1: 825: "J'ai vu un broulliard d'enfer...Oh ! Je suffoque, oh ! que c'est joli...oh ! comme ça se tient! Ô le centre. Et là, c'est une molécule. Le centre, c'est marveilleux. Le centre, oh ! il est beau. Oh là ! le centre. Ô le centre de Dieu. Et sa périphérie. Une périphérie n'a qu'un centre. Il y a des jardins. Ô la fatigue du mouvement. Je sens une périphéresthésie..." Nietzsche seems the most likely candidate for the character of the "German philosopher": within this chapter, Jarry includes the following exchange: "NOSOCOME: Logic is the hammer of reasoning. PYAST: Logic that kills." Nietzsche's last book published before his confinement in the asylum carried the full title *The Twilight of the Idols; or How to Philosophize with a Hammer* (1889).

And a few lines later: "Sengle was musing that he had said PERIPH-ERY and not *surface*..." (orthography original). This emphasis is curious; again we have two terms that are often used interchangeably: the *O.E.D.*, s.v. "periphery," gives under 2b: "More generally: the external boundary or *surface* of any space or body; something forming such a boundary."[23] Yet the *Grand Larousse* emphasizes the Greek etymology of the word *périphérie*: "Le grec *periphereia* est traduit exactement par le latin *circumferentia*. Circonférence, pourtour; surface extérieure." What Jarry is likely calling attention to here, particularly with his mention of "gardens," is that the Greek prefix *peri* ("around") is related to the word "paradise," of Arabic origin: see Webster, s.v. "paradise": "ME *paradis* > OFr. > LLat. *paradisus* > Gk. *paradeisos*, garden > Avestan *pairi-daEza-* [literally, "enclosed park"]: *pairi*, around + *daEza-*, wall (akin to Greek *peri* + *teichos* "wall"). The word "surface" is particularly significant in regard to Jarry's third recasting of the metaphor of the infinite sphere.

This third recasting occurs in the final chapter (41) of *Faustroll*, "Concerning the Surface of God," which falls at the end of Book VIII ("Ethernity"). It is in the *penultimate* chapter of *Faustroll* that Jarry seems to employ some of the techniques addressed by Cusanus in his *De docta ignorantia* (1440),[24] particularly in regard to *topology*. I use this twentieth-century term because it is more familiar than *analysis situs*, which was used almost exclusively up to the end of the 19th

---

23 My emphasis. The first entry is for the obsolete use of the word to describe "the strata of atmosphere enveloping the earth"; this is the *aer* and *aither* of the ancient Greeks, as well as the *ether* of physics up to and including the 19th century. Jarry puns on this idea with his neologism "Ethernity," which forms the title of the chapter of *Faustroll* that holds the final recasting of the metaphor of the infinite sphere; it is essentially a merging of terms for space and time: "ether" and "eternity." He cites his source as Aristotle's *De Caelo* ["On the Heavens," 1, iii].

24 See *Of Learned Ignorance*, Fr. Germain Heron, transl. (London: Routledge & Kegan Paul, 1954).

century,[25] and I employ it in its mathematical and geometrical sense as the "study of the properties of geometric configurations invariant under transformation by continuous mappings." Without delving into Cusanus' mathematical and geometrical demonstrations used as proof of the religious dogmas addressed in his text, I only cite here some of his chapter titles, which should give enough of an idea as to why Jarry would have found them useful: see for example Book I, Chapters XI, "Mathematics are a Very Great Help in the Understanding of Different Divine Truths," XV "The Infinite Line is a Triangle," XVI "The Infinite Triangle is a Circle and a Sphere," and XXIII "Analogy of the Infinite Sphere and the Actual Existence of God."

In Jarry's Chapter 40, simple geometric forms are apparently used to discuss the nature of God and the Trinity in largely Platonic terms. I say *apparently* for the following reason: in the first sentence, a "transcendent" God is described as "trigonal," in other words, "signified by a triangle" (as Jarry clarifies in Ch. 41), but in the second sentence, an "immanent" God is described as "trihedral," in an apparent attempt to add a "third-dimensional conjuration" to his discussion. But a "trihedra," or a three-sided polygon, is an impossible configuration, *at least in three-dimensional Euclidean space*; here the simplest form is the tetrahedron, or four-sided polygon, i.e. a pyramid, one of Plato's five regular

---

25 See Michael Monastyrsky, *Riemann, Topology, and Physics*, trans. James King and Victoria King; ed. R.O. Wells, Jr. (Boston: Birkhäuser, 1987) 9: "The term 'topology,' introduced by [Johann Benedict] Listing [1808-1882], became affixed to this branch of mathematics only at the beginning of our century; Riemann used exclusively the term 'analysis situs.'" Monastyrsky traces the phrase 'analysis situs' (analysis of *position*) to Leibniz; it also formed the title of a book by Henri Poincaré (1895), an early systematic treatment of topology. Earlier, in Chapter 38, one of two "telepathic letters" to Lord Kelvin, Jarry had written: "Now until the present moment I knew myself to be *elsewhere* than on earth..." (italics original) "But was I elsewhere in terms of date or of *position*, before or to the side, after or nearer? I was in that place where one finds oneself after having left time and space: *the infinite eternal*, Sir." (my italics).

polyhedra. Jarry then equates Man with the tetrahedron: "Therefore he is a solid, and God is spirit." That out of the way, he then writes explicitly at the end of the first paragraph of Chapter 41, "We shall content ourselves with two dimensions, so as to easily represent figures of plane geometry on a sheet of paper."

For what follows, one may, if one wishes, "hold to the letter of the story,"[26] as did another writer in his analysis,[27] but to do so is only to swallow Jarry's bait (recalling with my use of this metaphor that he was a masterful *angler*, a delightfully geometric term for a fisherman). Here we weave slowly, back and forth, between the realms of Empedocles and Pythagoras.[28] The latter is invoked twice: first in the mention of the Y of the "cross" of Anna Katherina Emmerick, an evocation of the *ypsilon* of the Pythagoreans[29] [not only the opposite (or *topological inversion*) of a triangle and related to the Greek character for the number 3, it reflected

26 "Nous nous en tenons, et avec raison, à la lettre de l'histoire, car il n'y a que la lettre qui soit littérature." ("We hold, and with reason, to the letter of the story, because it is only the letter which constitutes literature.") Jarry, *O.C.*, 2: 377.

27 Georges Petitfaux, "Sur l'ultime chapitre de Faustroll: De la Surface de Dieu," *Subsidia Pataphysica* 22, 67-69. Petitfaux, however, largely misinterprets Jarry's uses of the symbol for infinity (∞); Jarry is shrewdly making use of nineteenth-century developments in non-Euclidean geometry, which tend to set aside notions of an "actual" infinite in its own descriptions regarding the nature of space as "finite but unbounded." Additionally, Petitfaux's diagram, a graph of Jarry's equations, lacks the outer triangle described in Jarry's second paragraph as being "circumscribed around the traditional one," this perhaps for the sake of clarity (the diagram is described as "the initial figure"), but he seems to start with the Postulate, which begins only at Jarry's third paragraph. See also Brian Parshall, Leonard Scott, and Edward Cline, *Stratifying Endomorphism Algebras*, Memoirs of the American Mathematical Society 591 (Providence, RI: American Mathematical Society, 1996); as well as Brian Parshall and Jian-pan Wang, *Quantum Linear Groups*, MAMS 439 (1991).

28 See Philip, *Pythagoras*, 142: "Empedocles' surprising insights appear to be the result of acute observation and intuition. His tendency is not mathematical, and quantitative abstraction is quite foreign to the character of his thought, which is if anything *biological*" (my emphasis).

29 This is a Latinization of the Greek *upsilon*.

"the pattern of human life, the bottom leg being the age when one has been given over to neither virtues nor vices; the right branch good, the left evil"],[30] and secondly in the inclusion of the Pythagorean theorem ($a^2 = x^2 + y^2$; or "the square of the hypotenuse of a right triangle is equal to the sum of the squares of the other two sides"), *exactly in the middle* of his series of equations in the "Postulate" section. But regardless of whether one graphs out the equations to yield the geometric figure of concentric equilateral triangles surrounding a Y or not,[31] the various figures used in the equations [0 and ∞, and both positive (+ ; "Plus") and negative (—; "Minus") values for variables x and a, *as well as* for 0 and ∞][32] essentially *cancel each other out*, until one is left, at the

30 See Geoffroy Tory, *Champ Fleury* [New York: Johnson Reprint Corp., 1970 (Paris: 1529); see also this same title, George B. Ives, trans. and ed. (New York: The Grolier Club, 1927)] s.v. "Y." This book seems to have had quite an impact on Jarry's ideas regarding orthography and "the letter." But it holds much more as well; Tory conflates the Gallic Hercules (see my analysis of Dürer's engraving of this subject in Ch. I of the dissertation) with Hermes Trismegistus, making of him not only a great magician, but an astronomer and *founder of Paris*, by seeing in the name of the French city that of the region in Greece from which Hercules' troops were supposed to have come: Parrhasia. It was also Rabelais' source for his humorous discourse on the Limousin scholar who mutilated both French and Latin; Second Book, Ch. 6. See G. Mallary Masters, "Panurge at the Crossroads: A Mythopoetic Study of the Pythagroean Y in Rabelais's Satirical Romance (QL/33-34)," *Romance Notes* 15 (1973): 134-54; Masters also includes an illustration of Dürer's woodcut of the letter Y for comparison (it rather resembles a *lambda*; see here Jarry's "Pataphysics of Sophrotatos the Armenian," as above, n.7).
31 See Rabelais, Fourth Book, Ch. 55, "How Pantagruel, being at sea, heard various unfrozen words": "I have heard that a certain philosopher called Petron believed that there are several worlds touching one another as at the points of an equilateral triangle. The inner area of this triangle, he said, was the abode of truth and there lived the names and forms, the ideas and images of all things past and future. Outside this lies the Age—our secular world." Rabelais' source on Petron is Plutarch's *De defectu oraculorum* (422e), in which this "abode of truth" is further characterized as a "triangular 'Plain of Truth."
32 It seems likely that Jarry borrowed the notion of a "negative infinity" directly from Cusanus, who employs the phrase in relation to God in his *De docta ignorantia* (Heron trans., p. 94), but *not* to the universe (p. 70).

end of the Postulate, with "S = 0 $\sqrt{}$ 0 ."[33] (This self-cancellation is particularly evident in the final equation of the Corollary section, which simply results in a "proclamation of identity": $\infty = \infty$).[34] The square

---

33 See the article by science writer K.C. Cole, "The Question Is: What's Not Out There?," *Los Angeles Times* (2 September 1999): Metro section. Cole discusses the first law of thermodynamics, that of the conservation of energy, concluding as follows: "Most curious of all, adding up all the positive and negative energy in the universe gives you zero. The total positive and negative electric charge also adds up to zero. So does the total amount of matter and antimatter. All the quantities appear to exactly cancel out. When you add them up, all the fundamental attributes of the cosmos disappear into nothingness. This leads to an interesting speculation. The universe itself could have arisen from nothing at all. Cosmologists are searching for the answer. One of these days, they'll probably find it. Or not." I vote for "not." Evidently, "the answer" has been "known" for millenia. But by poets, not by scientists. It's simply a different kind of knowledge, *intuitive knowledge*, one that does not require such things as "proof." Nietzsche: "What must first be proven is worth little." *Twilight of the Idols*, "The Problem of Socrates." Jarry: "We do not know how to create out of nothingness, but we can do so out of chaos." *Days and Nights*, Book II, Ch. I (*O.C.*, 1: 770).

34 "The Bifurcation of Figurative Wit-Figurative wit can either spiritualize the body or corporealize the spirit. Originally, when man and the world still bloomed grafted to a single stem, this double trope was not a trope at all; man did not compare dissimilar things but *proclaimed their identity*. As with children, metaphors were simply forced synonyms of body and mind. In writing, pictographs came before letters; and so in speech, metaphor-insofar as it refers to relationships and not to objects-came first, and only gradually faded into the mere expression itself. Ensoulment and embodiment in the trope remained one and the same, because Self and World still coalesced. For this reason, every language, in its terms for things of the mind, is still a dictionary of withered metaphors." Jean Paul (Richter), *Vorshule der Ästhetik* (1804), section 50 (my emphasis). I have taken this from David R. Britt's note 3, p. 682, in his translation of Aby Warburg's *Die Erneuerung der heidnischen Antike*, published as *The Renewal of Pagan Antiquity* (Los Angeles: Getty Research Institute, 1999). For further reference, see Margaret R. Hale's *Horn of Oberon: John Paul Richter's School of Aesthetics* (Detroit: Wayne State UP, 1973), 131, etc.; it should be noted, however, that Hale's translation is fraught with errors, the most evident being her title, in which she "assumes" that English readers will understand her mistranslation of "Vorshule" ("School") as "Preschool." This is an important difference, in that it is largely only "before school" that one is still allowed to think intuitively; once one is indoctrinated into the symbolic order of "reading, writing, and 'rithmatic" all is lost; intuition is slowly crushed out of us until it only remains in limited form in artistic expression.

root of zero is, of course, zero; thus the Surface of God = 0. If Jarry were to follow Cusanus more closely, we might find some phrases here suggesting that 0 = circle = *ouroboros* = sphere, but it should be fairly clear by now that Jarry is simply reiterating the metaphor of the infinite sphere in mathematical terms unknown to the ancient Greeks. Zero, as is commonly known, was brought to the West by Arabic scribes in the 9th century, who borrowed it (along with basic numeral forms) from the Hindus; zero was not in widespread use in Europe until the thirteenth-century.[35] The symbol for infinity (∞) was first used in a seventeenth-century treatise on conic sections, John Wallis' *Arithmetica Infinitorum* of 1656.[36] Uses of both zero and infinity were "demonized" for some time following their introduction to the West, but eventually won over even the most defiant mathematician, and one would be hard-pressed now to find even one who so much as questions their use.

Jarry's "DEFINITION: God is the shortest distance between zero and infinity" is further qualified: in Euclidean space, as we are all taught, the shortest distance between two points is the straight line between them [in non-Euclidean space, as in nature (and as in Jarry's *writing*) *there are no 'straight lines'*]. So Jarry, who had earlier insisted that "the surface calculated is one line at the most," further reduces this line to a point ("But

---

35 The first use of zero as a place holder in positional base notation was due probably to Muhammad ibn Musa al-Khwarizmi (c. 780–850). Eastern Islam took over Indian arithmetic, and its basic numeral forms, complete with the zero, from the Hindus. This use of zero and the use of western Arabic (Gobar) numerals spread throughout Europe in the 10th century principally by the efforts of Gerbert de Aurillac (945–1003), who later became Pope Sylvester II. Before the adoption of positional base notation, zero, and the point, calculations such as multiplication, division, and root extraction had to be relegated to a handful of experts. By the 1100s the algorists, using base-10 notation, were successfully challenging the abacists (those using the abacus) in the speed and accuracy of calculations and had the "advantage" of a permanent written record of their results. [Paraphrased from several entries at *Encyclopaedia Britannica Online*].

36 Rudy Rucker, *Infinity and the Mind: The Science and Philosophy of the Infinite* (Boston: Birkhäuser, 1982), 1; 307 n.

God being without dimension is not a line…but a point")[37] just follow-ing the "proclamation of identity" mentioned above. "Therefore, *defini-tively*: GOD IS THE TANGENTIAL POINT BETWEEN ZERO AND INFINITY" (orthography original). Here we have a *topological inversion* of the *universe* as "an infinite sphere whose center is everywhere and whose circumference is nowhere." This is the *Sphairos* of the ancient Greek Eleatics, mentioned by Borges, further intuited in the cosmologi-cal poetry of Empedocles: God and the universe *are one and the same thing*, a pulsating, fluctuating, living, breathing, self-generating *biological* organism. We, its human "*in*habitants," here on the surface of the Earth for only a few million years at most, are mere specks of organic matter (Zarathustra's "dust") that formed in the glaucous waters of the puddle of its oceans on a particularly nice day, perhaps "the virgin, ever-return-ing, and beautiful today," of Mallarmé's poem[38]—soon (relatively), the sun may dry the puddle up (as has apparently happened on Mars, and perhaps Venus as well) and leave its inhabitants as "dessicated skeletons" to be reabsorbed, perhaps by certain forms of "rotatory friction," into its spherical surface, so similar to the dome of the Panthéon.[39] But *this* sur-face will revolve eternally, and the puddle will form again, only to dry up again…and again, and again.[40]

---

37 While this perhaps echoes Dante, both Protagoras and Democritus puzzled over whether the tangent to a circle meets it at a point or a line. Here is a fairly clear instance of what Jarry is often accused of doing throughout all of his work, positing a *reductio ad absurdum*.

38 Untitled poem from *Verse and Prose*, the fifteenth of Faustroll's *livres pairs* ("Le vierge, le vivace, et le bel aujourd'hui…"). I wonder if Jarry was as fooled as I was when first reading this poem; the first words seemed to suggest a "male virgin" until I realized that this is an adjectival modifier for the word "aujourd'hui" at the end of the line. Jarry was born on 9 September (1873), "The Feast of the Nativity of the Holy Virgin."

39 See *Maldoror*, Fifth Chant, second strophe; and the ultimate Chant, final strophe.

40 This is an allusion to the myth of eternal recurrence, which seems to have origi-nated with Pythagoras, and which is in many respects intrinsic to the metaphor of the infinite sphere. A discussion of this, however, is beyond the scope of even this wide-ranging essay; and besides, I'm out of *space*. Again, for fuller elaboration, see Chapter IV of the dissertation.

THE TIMELY TRANSFORMATION OF SUNDRY OBSERVATIONS IN AND METHODS AND PRINCIPLES OF DIVERS INDISPUTABLE MOTIONS OF BODIES INTO FIGGY NEW TONS OF PRINCIPIA ANIMATA GATE

David Daniels

I

Just as when you collect fumes of sulfur you hold a deacon over a burner so bodies in motion thrown up in the air will stay up in the air until able to descend meaningfully.

II

For as when you smell an odorless gas it is probably carbon monoxide so bodies in motion moving off a cliff will not fall if they do not look down.

III

Thus as blood flows down one leg and up the other many bodies in motion are able to assume a hurtling through the night locomotive shape if baited long enough.

IV

Just as mushrooms always grow in wet places because they look like umbrellas so bodies in motion turn blood red when furious and enjoy blasting appropriate smoke out their ears.

V

For as artificial insemination is when the farmer does it to the cow instead of the bull so a body in motion can become hard black plastic that rolls like a bowling ball and receives three mystical holes as its flabbergasted antagonists turn into pins.

VI

Thus as the pistol of a flower is its only protection against insects so your happy body in motion can pass through a solid wall newly painted to look like a tunnel entrance while your less fortunate body in motion will splat on the identical wall.

VII

Just as the supersaturated solution is the one which holds more than it can hold so a few cats and a few other select bodies in motion will frequently assume the shape of their containers.

VIII

For as the equator is a menagerie lion running around the middle of the earth so the average body in motion passing through solid matter will leave a perfect outline of its perimeter on any solid material facia still available.

IX

Thus as the vacuum is a large empty space where the Pope lives so the time required for a body in motion to fall off a building is greater than or equal to the time it takes for whatever body in motion that knocked it off to run down the stairs to catch or not catch the falling body in motion at the nadirical instant of its fall.

X

Just as one wears a condominium to prevent contraception so laws of gravity are negated for bodies in motion by higher levels of fear especially at panic intervals when feet turn into eggbeaters.

XI

For as a body in motion pulls the eye down over the nose to remove dust from the eye so stairs do not have to be visible to be ascended or descended or relaxed upon by self-certain bodies.

XII

Thus as it may be a misconception when a woman believes consuming alcohol has no affect on her fetus so when bodies in motion die large red or black X's appear on their eyes.

XIII

Just as when bodies in motion following their bliss that have achieved bliss will emit beep of gasoline machine so when bodies in motion are hungry their friends turn into hamburger.

XIV

For as sex, urination, and fecal elimination are unknown to bodies in motion so all eyeballs are always visible in the dark.

XV

Thus as a body in motion may be flattened to a thickness of one inch by a steamroller and regain its former shape or any other shape so a body in motion swallowing a spoon will often retain the shape of the spoon in a sideways reconfiguration of its throat.

XVI
Just as a body in motion may fill with air and expand into explosion then regain its former state so bodies in motion may ricochet off walls indefinitely into ever decreasing sizes.

XVII
For as when bodies in motion sneeze feathers come off them or large buildings collapse so a body in motion's parts separated from each other during explosion will reassemble in various arrangements albeit usually in their original arrangement.

XVIII
Thus as a body in motion turned inside out loses all surface feature and only dusk filled outline remains so a body in motion in a state of infatuation is often able to float as small singing bodies in motion fly around its head chirping spring song.

XVIX
Just as the eyeballs of bodies in motion assume spirals when hypnotized and dollar signs will appear in their eyes when greed is mentioned so a light bulb may appear over the heads of bodies in motion when an idea is more to them than mildly apparent.

XX
For as bodies in motion are able to run under and through solid ground freely so the teeth and eyeballs of bodies in motion can leap in and out for exorbitant distances.

XXI
Thus as bodies in motion exhibit a fluoroscopic skeleton when placing a finger in an electric socket so they may react to severe vicissitudes by seizure into an extremely tight wired coil.

XXII
Just as when bodies in motion take in excess water and water jets
rocket out their ears so if a like body in motion is bullet riddled water
will spout out of its bullet holes.

XXIII
For as bodies in motion are able to stop bullets from leaving a gun
barrel by sticking their finger in so if morally superior they may draw a
hole on a wall and a lady, a tiger and an entire Roman circus newly con-
verted to Christianity will parade out endlessly.

XXIV
Thus as a falling safe flattens a body in motion only if the body in
motion believes the safe is able to flatten it so extravagantly inner
directed bodies in motion with lengthy auricle, extensive incisor, and
posterior of cotton can never be killed.

XXV
Therefore as bodies in meta motion germinate when they become
naturalized Germans and then snake bitten rape themselves in blankets
for shock so as speed increases bodies in motion will divide up into
more than several different yet equal body locations at once and yelp
stars shine bright on shatter light boop boop a doop I taut I taw a put-
tee cat zipidy doo dah quoth the raven eat my shorts which way did he
go George thanks for inviting me to your birthday party Donald don't
make me kick your ass this sucks change it you mean widdle wabbit I
fights with the Finnish cause they eats me kïnïsh. Thee. The. The. That's
they're here to save the world, folks.

"Beyond Laughter": Nietzsche and Pataphysics

Anthony Enns

The science of "pataphysics" was outlined by Alfred Jarry in his book *Exploits and Opinions of Dr. Faustroll, Pataphysician*, which was written in 1898 but not published until 1911, four years after Jarry's death. Due to Jarry's use of humor, as well as the fact that he attended Henri Bergson's classes for two years at the lycée Henri IV, many critics have attempted to employ Bergson's theory of laughter as a philosophical foundation for pataphysics. Bergson outlined this theory in his book *Le Rire*, which was first published in 1899, the year after Jarry wrote *Dr. Faustroll*, and some critics, such as Roger Shattuck, have used Bergson's theory as a key to understanding not only Jarry's work, but also the zeitgeist of late nineteenth-century Paris. It is clear from Jarry's own writings, however, that he strongly disagreed with many of Bergson's ideas and in this paper I will attempt to explain these disagreements. I suggest that the relationship between pataphysics and humor is better understood through a consideration of Friedrich Nietzsche's theory of laughter. Nietzsche's theory offers a more useful context for understanding pataphysics because his notions of art, play, and intuition are all bound together by laughter, and unlike Bergson, who describes laughter as a group effort to control and subdue those who do not conform to society, Nietzsche's theory maintains the promise that laughter can be used to expose the underlying fictions which structure reality. Nietzsche, like Jarry, attempts to use laughter as a way of criticizing and resisting these fictions, thus endowing humor with a liberatory and subversive potential which remains absent in Bergson's work.

Jarry defines pataphysics as "the science of imaginary solutions, which symbolically attributes the properties of objects, described by their virtuality, to their lineaments."[1]

An example of the way pataphysics questions scientific laws can be seen when Dr. Faustroll discusses the law of gravity: "Instead of formulating the law of the fall of a body toward a center, how far more apposite would be the law of the ascension of a vacuum toward a periphery, a vacuum being considered a unit of non-density, a hypothesis far less arbitrary than the choice of a concrete unit of positive density such as *water*?"[2] According to Faustroll, pataphysics is a science that acknowledges scientific laws as essentially arbitrary and based on accidental data, its only general principle being that there are no general principles.

Because it is a science without general principles, pataphysics may remind contemporary readers of Michel Foucault's preface to *The Order of Things*:

> This book first arose out of a passage in Borges, out of the laughter that shattered...all the familiar landmarks of my thoughts...breaking up all the ordered surfaces and all the planes with which we are accustomed to tame the wild profusion of existing things...This passage quotes a 'certain Chinese encyclopaedia' in which it is written that 'animals are divided into: (a) belonging to

1 Alfred Jarry, *Exploits & Opinions of Dr. Faustroll, Pataphysician*, trans. Simon Watson Taylor (Boston: Exact Change, 1996), 22.
2 Ibid.

the Emperor, (b) embalmed, (c) tame, (d) sucking pigs, (e) sirens, (f) fabulous, (g) stray dogs, (h) included in the present classification, (i) frenzied, (j) innumerable, (k) drawn with a very fine camelhair brush, (l) *et cetera*, (m) having just broken the water pitcher, (n) that from a long way off look like flies.' In the wonderment of this taxonomy, the thing we apprehend in one great leap, the thing that, by means of the fable, is demonstrated as the exotic charm of another system of thought, is the limitation of our own.[3]

What Foucault finds remarkable about this taxonomy is that it is a list of exceptions which are being presented as a totalizing body of knowledge, and what we immediately "apprehend" in this "fable" is that all of our own systems of classification are essentially performing the same function: they are fictional constructs which hopelessly attempt "to tame the wild profusion of existing things."

The similarity between Foucault and Jarry is not only that they both expose scientific systems of knowledge as essentially fictional and arbitrary, but also that this process is performed through the use of humor. According to Foucault, for example, it was the "laughter" which accompanied his revelation "that shattered...all the familiar landmarks of my thoughts." In other words, humor itself seems to activate the subversive potential in Borges' story. Pataphysics has similarly been described as an essentially humorous concept, which also contains a serious and subversive potential. In his pamphlet *Au Seuil de la 'Pataphysique*, for example, Shattuck writes, "The comic and the serious are identical: the comic is the serious hiding behind the mask of craziness; the serious taken seriously is inexorably crazy."[4] In other

---

3 Michel Foucault, *The Order of Things* (New York: Vintage Books, 1994), xv.

words, the humor of pataphysics is merely a mask, which conceals a serious and subversive potential hiding underneath, while the seriousness of normative science is similarly a mask, which conceals its underlying craziness. This blurring of the comic and the serious is even more pronounced in René Daumal's 1928 essay "Pataphysics and the Revelation of Laughter," in which he argues that "pataphysics is not simply a joke," but rather "the only human expression of despair."[5] Like Shattuck, Daumal suggests that pataphysical thought moves back and forth between the comic and the serious: "[T]he comic appearance of pataphysical reasoning...seems grotesque, then at second glance seems to contain a hidden meaning, then upon closer examination appears *decidedly* grotesque, then again more deeply meaningful, etc."[6] In the end, however, Daumal argues that the subversive potential of pataphysics to "negate" and "reject" ideas through laughter is ultimately nihilistic, and he refers to it as a "[d]evouring, gluttonous thought, with respect for nothing, believing in and pledging allegiance to no one, brutal with its own evidence in defiance of all logic."[7]

Daumal's characterization of pataphysics as comic nihilism is precisely the sort of interpretation which the Collège de 'Pataphysique attempted to undo in their 1958 advertisement "What Is 'Pataphysics?":

> [I]t is not a question, as some simple minds who take Jarry for a satirist seem to think, of denouncing human activities and cosmic reality; it is not a question of promoting a mocking pessimism or a corrosive nihilism. On the contrary. It is a question of discovering the perfect harmony in all things, and through this harmony the

---

4 Roger Shattuck, *Au Seuil de la 'Pataphysique* (Paris: Collège de 'Pataphysique, 1962), 9.
5 René Daumal, "Pataphysics and the Revelation of Laughter," in *The Powers of the Word: Selected Essays and Notes 1927-1943*, ed. and trans. Mark Polizzoti (San Francisco: City Lights Books, 1991), 15-16.
6 Ibid, 18-19.
7 Ibid, 17.

profound concordance between men's minds…[T]hese activities…correspond to a general viewpoint and an entirely new psychology. Beyond laughter, and even beyond smiling perhaps.[8]

In other words, pataphysics does not shatter systems of thought with the abandon of an anarchist, but rather its goal is empowerment and enlightenment, a "profound concordance between men's minds," which is "beyond laughter." The goals of pataphysics should therefore not be confused with those of a practical jokester, who simply wants to mock and ridicule, but rather its theoretical foundation seems to resemble the work of Nietzsche, who was dedicated to shattering systems of thought but also wary of such practices devolving into nihilism. In his essay "On Truth and Falsity in an Extramoral Sense," for example, Nietzsche describes the impulse behind tearing down the illusions which masquerade in society as "truth":

> This impulse seeks for itself a new realm of action and another river-bed, and finds it in…*Art*. This impulse constantly confuses the rubrics and cells of the ideas, by putting up new figures of speech, metaphors, metonymies; it constantly shows its passionate longing for shaping the existing world of waking man as motley, irregular, inconsequentially incoherent, attractive, and eternally new as the world of dream is.[9]

Like art, the practice of pataphysics—the science of the particular—exposes the world as "irregular" and "incoherent," which makes

---

8 "What is 'Pataphysics?'" (Paris: Collège de 'Pataphysique, 1958).
9 Friedrich Nietzsche, "On Truth and Falsity in an Extramoral Sense," in *Friedrich Nietzsche on Rhetoric and Language*, ed. Sander L. Gilman, Carole Blair and David J. Parent (New York: Oxford University Press, 1989), 188.

it possible, in Nietzsche's words, for the intellect to be "no longer led by ideas but by intuitions."[10]

Nietzsche's notion of laughter as a tool for shattering systems of thought is outlined in *Thus Spake Zarathustra* (1883), where he introduces an opposition between "laughter of the herd" and "laughter of the height." "Laughter of the herd" refers to the laughter of mobs and crowds, and Nietzsche describes this laughter at the beginning of the book, when the crowd rejects Zarathustra's teachings: "How they look on me and laugh: and while they laugh they hate me. There is ice in their laughter."[11] Zarathustra later returns this gesture with his own laughter, which he calls the "laughter of the height": "I will soon bring your hiding-places to the light: therefore do I laugh in your face my laughter of the height."[12] Nietzsche's concept of the "laughter of the height" reappears later in the book, where Zarathustra encounters a shepherd choking on a snake. Zarathustra encourages the shepherd to bite the snake, and after taking his advice, the shepherd jumps up and begins to laugh: "No longer a shepherd, no longer a man—but one transfigured, light-encompassed, one that *laughed!*"[13] Therefore, in contrast to the "laughter of the herd," which is associated with scorn and ridicule, the "laughter of the height" is associated with freedom and transcendence.

Several critics have already commented on Nietzsche's "laughter of the height." Pete Gunter, for example, claims that this form of laughter "expresses the attainment of desire, while the other expresses some measure of frustration."[14] John Lippitt also points out that "laughter of the herd" is always directed from a group onto an estranged outsider, while "the laughter of the height...involves as an important element

---

10 Ibid, 190.
11 Friedrich Nietzsche, *Thus Spake Zarathustra*, trans. A. Tille (New York: Everyman's Library, 1933), 10.
12 Ibid.
13 Ibid, 143.
14 Pete A. Gunter, "Nietzschean Laughter," *Sewanee Review* 76 (1968): 505.

laughing at…one's own existence."[15] Lippitt adds that "the person who attains the height can laugh at 'all tragedies, real or imaginary.' From the vantage-point of the height, there is nothing that cannot be amusing, and the ultimate joke is life itself."[16] Lippitt concludes that Nietzsche's "laughter of the height" is therefore an "affirmation of suffering," and that by laughing at themselves the higher men have a greater perspective on their own suffering.[17] However, neither Gunter nor Lippitt acknowledge the ways in which Nietzsche repeatedly employs metaphors of height, perspective, and distance in order to illustrate a deeper awareness of the fictions which structure one's perceptions of reality. For example, Lippitt is correct in noting that Zarathustra calls for the higher men to laugh at themselves: "Learn to laugh at yourselves, as one should laugh!"[18] However, he ignores the fact that Zarathustra later repeats this command in a slightly altered form: "Learn to laugh beyond yourselves!"[19] By adding the word "beyond," Nietzsche references an earlier passage, in which Zarathustra climbs a mountain and reflects on the relationship between perspective and knowledge. In this passage, height carries the potential of leading Zarathustra *beyond* himself by allowing him to "look down upon myself" from above, which allows him to see "the ground and background of all things."[20] This connection between height and knowledge also echoes *The Gay Science* (1882), in which Nietzsche discusses the difference between looking up at a mountain from below and looking down from its summit. Nietzsche argues that mountains make the landscape seem charming and magical, but when you look down from the summit, "the mountain itself and the whole

---

15 John Lippitt, "Nietzsche, Zarathustra and the Status of Laughter," *British Journal of Aesthetics* 32.1 (1992): 44.

16 Ibid.

17 Ibid, 48.

18 Nietzsche, *Zarathustra*, 258.

19 Ibid, 260.

20 Ibid, 138.

landscape around us, below us, have lost their magic."[21] Nietzsche compares this disillusionment to the process of gaining self-knowledge: "Perhaps you know some people near you who must look at themselves only from a distance in order to find themselves at all tolerable or attractive and invigorating. Self-knowledge is strictly inadvisable for them."[22] In both passages, height compresses distance and implies closeness and intimate knowledge. The perspective that height allows, therefore, is not the ability to see things from a safe distance, but rather to penetrate the empty façade of reality, such as the charm of a landscape, and to see instead "the ground and background of all things."

Nietzsche also employs height as a metaphor for knowledge in the essay "On Truth and Falsity in an Extramoral Sense," where he claims that "truths are illusions" which have become so "fixed" and "intensified" from "long usage" that "one has forgotten that they *are* illusions."[23] Nietzsche also refers to man's faith in truth as a "prison," and he once again uses height to describe the process of realizing the inherent artificiality of truth: a man looking down from above is not only able to see beyond the "prison walls of this faith," but he is also able to see the prison for what it is. Nietzsche compares this viewer from the height to an artist or "freed intellect," who is "no longer led by ideas but by intuitions," and is thus able to recognize the absence of any fixed truths. This discovery is reenacted through the building of a temporary, artificial structure, which the artist destroys and then reassembles "ironically, pairing the strangest, separating the nearest items."[24] This kind of art, which ironically makes fun of ideas and draws attention to its own artifice, is precisely what Nietzsche calls for in his introduction

---

21 Friedrich Nietzsche, *The Gay Science*, trans. Walter Kaufmann (New York: Vintage, 1974), 89-90.
22 Ibid, 90.
23 Nietzsche, "Truth and Falsity," 180.
24 Ibid, 190.

to *The Gay Science*: "a mocking, light, fleeting, divinely untroubled, divinely artificial art."[25] And the essence of this art is laughter.

Jarry's concept of pataphysics, designed to reveal the underlying fiction behind scientific theories and systems of classification, clearly reflects Nietzsche's notion that art should reveal the impossibility of fixed truths. Like Nietzsche, Jarry does not embrace comic nihilism, but rather laughter. Despite these obvious similarities, however, the relationship between pataphysics and humor is more often explained using Bergson's theory of laughter. Shattuck, for example, uses Bergson's distinction between irony and humor to describe the philosophical foundation of Jarry's work.[26] It is not surprising that Shattuck would attempt to draw a connection between the works of Jarry and Bergson because Bergson was one of Jarry's teachers at the lycée Henry IV, and Jarry attended Bergson's class on the history of philosophy two consecutive years. Although Bergson published *Le Rire* after Jarry wrote *Dr. Faustroll*, it is also clear from Jarry's notebooks that Bergson was developing his theory of laughter in those classes. However, a closer look at Jarry's disagreements with Bergson will show that there is a fundamental difference between Bergson's theory of laughter and the practice of pataphysics.

Bergson defines the comic as "something mechanical encrusted on the living."[27] In other words, "the attitudes, gestures and movements of the human body are laughable in exact proportion as that body reminds us of a mere machine."[28] Repetition and similarity, according to Bergson, also suggest something mechanical: "Two faces that are alike, although neither of them excites laughter by itself, make us laugh when

---

25 Nietzsche, *Gay Science*, 37.

26 Roger Shattuck, *The Banquet Years* (New York: Harcourt, Brace and Company, 1958), 26-27.

27 Henri Bergson, *Laughter: An Essay on the Meaning of the Comic*, trans. Cloudesley Brereton and Fred Rothwell (New York: Macmillan, 1911), 37.

28 Ibid, 29.

together, on account of their likeness."[29] Bergson adds that a public speaker who repeats the same gesture is comical in a similar way. By pointing out all of the qualities which are unnatural or artificial, Bergson places "the rigid, the ready-made, the mechanical, in contrast with the supple, the ever-changing and the living"[30] Like Nietzsche's "laughter of the height," therefore, Bergson's laughter seems to reveal that which is artificial, false, and ultimately oppressive to life.

In his book *Jokes and Their Relation to the Unconscious*, Sigmund Freud attempts to fit Bergson's definition of the comic into his own theory of laughter. Laughter, according to Freud, is associated with the release of psychical expenditures, and the pleasure that laughter produces "corresponds to the psychical expenditure that is saved."[31] Mechanical gestures and movements produce laughter, therefore, because they allow us to conserve psychic energy: "Everything has taught us that every living thing is different from every other and calls for a kind of expenditure by our understanding; and we find ourselves disappointed if, as a result of complete conformity or deceptive mimicry, we need make no fresh expenditure."[32] Freud adds, however, that by "disappointment" he also means "relief," and "the expenditure which has become superfluous is discharged by laughter."[33] It is through this notion of laughter as the pleasurable release of psychic tension that Freud explains the close connection between jokes and dreams: Laughter, like dreams, allows for the healthy release of repressed thoughts and inhibitions.

Freud's association of laughter with the process of dreams and intuition seems to echo Nietzsche's claim that the artist, who is "no longer

---

29 Ibid, 34.
30 Ibid, 130.
31 Sigmund Freud, *Jokes and Their Relation to the Unconscious*, ed. and trans. James Strachey (New York: Norton, 1963), 118.
32 Ibid, 209.
33 Ibid.

led by ideas but by intuitions," shapes "the existing world of waking man as motley, irregular, inconsequentially incoherent, attractive, and eternally new as the world of dream is." However, rather than activating the play of ideas and the dream logic implicit in the comic, Bergson repeatedly claims that laughter actually stifles creativity and returns to pure logic. Laughter, for Bergson, is a "*social gesture*," which "restrains eccentricity" by inspiring "fear," and it can thus be interpreted as a means for society to pursue the "utilitarian aim of general improvement."[34] While the "comic character" appears similar to Nietzsche's higher man, who refuses to conform to the herd, Bergson only conceives of laughter as the means by which society disciplines him, such as the icy "laughter of the herd" which the mob uses against Zarathustra. Bergson even claims that "laughter is always the laughter of a group."[35] In other words, rather than seeing the potentially liberating power of laughter, Bergson only recognizes laughter as a tool for socialization.

Bergson's notion of laughter as a social corrective is clearly influenced by Charles Baudelaire's 1855 essay "The Essence of Laughter," where he argues that laughter stems from an individual's conception of his own superiority, such that it is always directed towards others. In other words, there is something inherently cruel and arrogant about laughter. He provides the example of people laughing when they see someone take a fall: "[i]t is not the victim of a fall who laughs at his own misfortune."[36] However, Baudelaire immediately adds that this is not true if the victim "happens to be a philosopher, in other words a being who, as the result of long habit, has acquired the power rapidly to

---

34 Bergson, 20.

35 Ibid, 6.

36 Charles Baudelaire, "The Essence of Laughter and More Especially of the Comic in Plastic Arts," in *The Essence of Laughter and Other Essays, Journals, and Letters*, ed. Peter Quennell, trans. Gerard Hopkins (New York: Meridian Books, 1956), 117-8.

become two persons at one and the same time, and can bring to bear on what happens to *himself* the disinterested curiosity of a spectator."[37] Like Nietzsche's higher men, Baudelaire claims that these philosophers are "closer to the state of childhood."[38] He therefore introduces a second category of the comic, which he refers to as the absolutely comic, which "has in it something profound, axiomatic and primitive, which more closely relates it to innocence and to absolute joy than does the laughter occasioned by the comedy of manners."[39] In contrast to Bergson's theory of laughter, Baudelaire maintains a notion of the comic that, like Nietzsche's, is tied to playful creativity, joyful wisdom, and the importance of intuition over ideas.

Because Jarry was a student of Bergson's and because there are elements of Bergson's theory that are similar to Nietzsche's, it is easy to see how critics could confuse Jarry's notion of humor with Bergson's. However, it is clear from Jarry's own writing that he disagreed with Bergson. For example, in *La Chandelle Verte* Jarry writes, "Laughter is not, we believe, only that which has been defined by our excellent professor of philosophy at the lycée Henri IV: the feeling of surprise. We suggest he should add: the impression of revealed truth—which surprises, like all unexpected discoveries."[40] Although Jarry acknowledges that Bergson is correct in defining laughter as the surprise, he immediately criticizes Bergson for ignoring the power of laughter that accomplishes or accompanies discovery. Therefore, rather than conceiving of laughter as a gesture that simply confirms what is already known, as Bergson does, Jarry defines it as a revelation of the unexpected and the unknown. Rather than conceiving of laughter as a gesture that imposes some fixed notion of truth, Jarry sees it provide a

---

37 Ibid, 118.
38 Ibid.
39 Ibid, 121.
40 Alfred Jarry, *La Chandelle Verte* (Paris: Livre de Poche, 1969), 301.

clearer perception of the existing world. Jarry holds that "laughter is born out of the discovery of the contradictory."[41] Unlike Bergson, who conceives of laughter as suppressing contradiction and reinforcing uniformity, Jarry's laughter is released when contradiction is discovered. In other words, laughter is produced when one realizes that there is a difference between what something is and what it is supposed to be, which echoes Nietzsche's notion of art as recognizing the world as "irregular" and "inconsistent."

Catherine Stehlin, in her study of Jarry's notes from Bergson's lectures, points out that Jarry's philosophical interests often diverge from Bergson's: "Jarry's 'philosophical' preoccupations are not entirely due to the influence of Bergson's course."[42] She also notes that Jarry contradicts one of the fundamental principles of Bergson's philosophy: "la durée," or "duration." According to Stehlin,

> Bergson never stops proclaiming the absolute difference between these "two infinities" (the nature of time is qualitative, the nature of space quantitative); therefore he insists on the subjective character of duration, and doesn't hesitate to be indignant against the "geometry" of time…Jarry, as if he knew nothing about it, or better, as if the bergsonian conception of "fluid" time (which he calls "viscous") seemed to him outdated and "poetically banal," "naively" declares that "space and time are commensurable."[43]

In other words, Jarry's seemingly naïve declaration that "space and time are commensurable" represents a resistance to Bergson's concept of "duration," which he finds "outdated" and "poetically banal."

---

41 As quoted in Shattuck, *Banquet Years*, 184-185.
42 Catherine Stehlin, "Jarry, Le Cours Bergson et la Philosophie," *Europe* 623/624 (Mars/Avril 1981): 40.
43 Ibid, 39.

Although Bergson does not mention the concept of duration in *Le Rire*, François Boullant suggests that laughter, for Bergson, may represent the very absence of duration: "Perhaps laughter is a brief moment of 'forgetting' duration."[44] The fact that one of the key elements of the comic is surprise indicates another possible way in which something mechanical is imposed upon the living, or, in this case, of something spatial imposed upon the temporal: The comic is a brief moment of geometric time, which laughter quickly purges. By placing space and time on the same plane, Jarry threatens the basic law of Bergson's philosophy, thereby tearing down, as Nietzsche suggests, the "prison walls of faith" which this principle implies.

These disagreements with Bergson, as well as the striking similarities between Jarry's notion of laughter and Nietzsche's "laughter of the height," suggest that pataphysics owes a greater debt to Nietzsche's writings than to Bergson's. The resemblance is marked enough to provoke one to wonder whether Jarry read Nietzsche or whether this similarity is coincidental. The latter answer would seem to be more in keeping with the central tenets of their philosophies, as any act of explaining correspondences would necessarily involve the imposition of some fictional truth upon accidental data. However, Stehlin offers a causal connection to explain their similarities: after pointing out Jarry's differences with Bergson, she adds that Jarry was more influenced by a professor of philosophy at the lycée de Rennes named M. Bourdon, who created a scandal by teaching the works of Friedrich Nietzsche as early as 1889, before Nietzsche had been translated into French.[45] Although it remains unknown which of his works Jarry studied, Nietzsche's influence on the development of pataphysics is unmistakable.

---

44 François Boullant, *Henri Bergson: Le Rire* (Paris: Bertrand-Lacoste, 1994), 61.
45 Stehlin, 40.

T][ime][ext. Travel

MEZ (Mary-Anne Breeze)

wavz ov motion, prepulsed in2 ah prepack-aged nuance n fold.ed
in2 strait

jacketted linez of thort…
we all falle pr.eye 2 the move, the jolt: others poke n prik whilst the
motion c[l]atchez, a thread thort strung b-tween the wurdz, n-
cou.rage.ment
a.live…
wot about the ebb? the spacez fallinge cy[borg]lent, the mot[ez of
creatiff
dust]ion caught in a down.ward[inge offe the d-monz] tr.end[ov
the spurge,
the peake], re-readee 4 the move, the shifte……

****
thizz is not a re:sponse
thiz is knot a re[aper]sponse
****

repli 2 sendah pleaze
[no mezzinezz here; no public [t]outin, no removal ov
respons[abiliteez]e,
no actualitee ov the concrete]
[i hurtle bi, rapid machinez lumberin thru speed, a stand-uppe vertical
ope.rat[ion].ore required, 1 d-signed 2 withstand the n-evet.able,
the
s[iren][pud]endah]

✶✶✶
!!!STOP!!!
…& s.eye
✶✶

strainz cap.tored, w[h]it[e]nezz a bench.mark[N scrawl n shift],
shere
act.u.allz d-nighed, otherz caught [s]here 2:
A machine that cuts sheet metal by passing a blade through it
(physics) a deformation of an object in which parallel planes remain
parallel but are shifted in a direction parallel to themselves
Shear the fibre from

✶✶✶
[grasping - @ - straw- mean-ingez]
[narratiff string requ.ire.ment[ioned here at forced wille]]
✶✶

[i lick at three]
waves of motion::

[pulsing before as well as after, present past and future joined in a thump
of matter designed to carbon copy, replicate, and breed/bleed]
prepulsed into a prepackaged nuance::
[should it be bound?restrained?forwarded?]
and folded into straight-jacket lines of thought…
[ah, theory, maybe Sartre could explain, or perhaps one of the others,
filled up with words designed to make it clear, masked only by the rhythm/the largess/the concept]
We all fall prey to the move, the jolt: others poke and prick through ashes
designed to provoke, or tracts designed to placate. Whilst the motion
catches a thread, the thought may be strung between the words, encouraged,
or artificially rewired as a conduit for life…
And what about the ebb? The spaces falling silent, the motes of creative
dust and motion caught in a downward trend, the warding off of data demons
not enough to stop the spurge or the peak, the shift…

****

this is like knot theory
this is not a response
****

Reply to your sender, please.
[Don't get messy here; don't publically tout, don't remove your responses,
don't actualise the concrete]

[I hurtle by, my rapid machinez lumbering through speed, a stand-
up
vertical operator required, one designed to withstand the inevitable,
the
sender.]

Telepathic Letter to Alfred Jarry

Brisbane di Milo

> Man today, stripped of myth, stands famished
> among all his pasts and must dig frantically for roots,
> be it among the most remote antiquities. What does
> our great historical hunger signify, our clutching about
> us of countless other cultures, our consuming desire for
> knowledge, if not the loss of myth, of a mythic home,
> the mythic womb?

> ——Friedrich Nietzsche, *The Birth of Tragedy*,
> Section 23.

Dear Mr. Jarry,

Having read your columns in *La Revue blanche*, and much of your published work to date,[1] I have noticed your strong interest in sporting

---

1. It will be noted that the "date" of this letter is left entirely unclear; references are made to works published and events that occurred long after Jarry's "death," or his transition to the immortality of "eternal life." It is curious to note that Marcel Duchamp's epitaph, "D'ailleurs c'est toujours les autres qui meurent," ("Anyway, it's always the others who die") seems to echo Jarry's words in a letter to Rachilde written a few months before his own demise: "La mort n'est que les autres…" ("Death is only for the others…") Alfred Jarry *Œuvres Complètes*, 3 vols. (Paris: Gallimard, Bibliothèque de la Pléiade, 1988) 3: 659. [Hereafter *O.C.*]

activities, primarily those of bicycling and fishing, but also acrobatics, gymnastics and other related physical exertions, largely in respect to the individual, often with an angle toward ancient practice. You make little mention of team sports however (despite ancient origins going as far back as at least Sparta, or perhaps even Egypt), except in terms of multiple-seat cycling, although your many allusions to the writings of François Rabelais suggest that you are aware of his long list of children's games in Chapter XXII of his First Book, and by extension Pieter Bruegel the Elder's painting of a similar theme, both of which include group sports. There are intimations in your work that you may also know of the ancient ballgame called *tlachtli* played by the Zapotecs in the hemisphere from which I write (which seems to have originated with the Olmec, the so-called "rubber people," perhaps distant relatives of your *palotins*), a game in which it seems that the *winners* were sacrificed to the gods (as implied in your article of 1 August 1901,[2] you seem acutely aware that your Celtic ancestors also employed similar practices, death for those cultures being something less to be feared than *welcomed*). For these and other reasons, I write to inform you now of a group sport played here in the United States, of which there is mention in our own journals as early as 1823, but which probably dates to at least as early as the mid-seventeenth-century. This is the so-called "national pastime" of our nation, the game of *baseball*, probably derived from a similar game played in Britain called *rounders*. It is a sport which I think you will find of great interest, for several reasons which will be spelled out below.

The game is played by two opposing teams of *nine* players each, often with reserves; the teams alternate between offensive and defensive positions, the former being called *batters*, the latter *fielders*. It is played outdoors on a playing field that is divided for convenience into two areas called the *infield* and the *outfield*. I think you will find it curious that the

---

2 "Les Sacrifices humains du 14 juillet," *O.C.* (1987), 2: 310-311.

infield is referred to as a *diamond*, although it is laid out in the form of a square rather than a lozenge, each corner holding a flat white *base* (hence the first syllable of the name of the game). Actually, it is in the form of a *quincunx*, which, as you well know, is a word derived from the Latin for "five twelfths" (a phrase which bears distant echoes of the *dodecahedron*, in addition to the Roman coin called the *as*) and which refers to an arrangement of five things with one at each corner of a square or parallelogram and one in the center. There are intimations in your occasional references to the work of the poet Franc-Nohain that you may have read Sir Thomas Browne's famous *paired books*,[3] *Urn Burial* and *The Garden of Cyrus*, in which the author specifically refers to the quincunx in relation to Cyrus the Great's tree plantation, *speculating* that the pattern may have originated in "the Prototype and originall of Plantations," the Garden of Eden, "since even in Paradise it self, the tree of knowledge was placed in the middle of the Garden," a *reflection*, as you have apparently noted, of the ancient mythological trope of the "world tree." (I have noticed that both you and Mr. Pierre Bonnard often depict your Mr. Ubu with a single leaf upon the peak of his conical head, suggesting a withered example of such a tree, *à la* Irminsul, atop a "world mountain.") While no trees are allowed on a baseball field, the center of the diamond does hold a small hill or rise called a *mound*. This is *not exactly* the same as that which holds Ubu in the 1901 version of your play, nor is it exactly Calvary, nor Montmarte, nor "Le Fouzi-Yama,"[4] but you will

---

3 See Jarry's list of the 27 *livres pairs* (*O.C.,* 1: 661) that Dr. Faustroll takes with him on his celestial journey to the seven visible planets, or the "blessed isles" of Greek myth; the number 27 is most often equated with the books of the New Testament, but it is also the number of companions that accompany the Celtic hero Bran on his *immram* or sea-voyage to the mythical Celtic *Otherworld*. This can be found in the Irish Celtic *Navigation of Bran, Son of Febal*. It will be noted that while some of Faustroll's *livres pairs* are paradisaical in nature ("Garden of Cyrus"), and some are infernal ("Urn Burial"), several exhibit characteristics of both. As the members of Monty Python suggested in their film "The Life of Brian," there are numerous links between the legendary lives of Christ, King Arthur, and the Irish Celtic Bran (the name Brian stems from Bran).

4 *O.C.,* 2: 539.

recognize that it seems to resonate from the same source,[5] judging from your article of this title in the July 1905 issue of *Poesia*,[6] and other persistent allusions in your work to worldwide mythology.

In fact, as you know (here your 1 June 1901 review of Veuve Pierrel's book *Éternite*),[7] this arrangement seems to echo ancient

---

5 Perhaps this is why the game of baseball has become so popular in Japan.

6 The editors of the Pléiade Jarry (2: 927n) suggest that the spelling of the title of this piece is "personal" to Jarry, but he only echoes that employed by Edmond de Goncourt in his biography of Hokusai, the master painter and printmaker of *ukiyo-e* ("pictures of the floating world"), whose famous print series "Thirty-six Views of Mount Fuji," published between 1826 and 1833, marked the pinnacle of Japanese color woodblock landscape. See Edmond de Goncourt, *Hokousaï* (Paris: G. Charpentier et E. Fasquelle, 1896), Chapter XXXII, "Les Trente-six vues du Fouzi-Yama, les Cascades, les Ponts," and Chapter XLII, "Les Cent vues du Fouzi-Yama." [See now Matthi Forrer, *Hokusai* (New York: Rizzoli, 1988) with E. de Goncourt texts in translation.] This oblique and subtle allusion to the work of Hokusai is typical of Jarry, and is undoubtedly meant to signal the strong attention to mythological subjects in the work of the Japanese master. *Ukiyo-e* is most often considered as a "style" or "school" by art historians, but its translation as "pictures of the floating world" (Goncourt addresses this phrase in his book) surely appealed to Jarry in regard to his knowledge of Celtic myth, with its constant evocations of a mythological *Otherworld* and its misty or "watery" realms. The mountain's name, of Ainu origin, means "everlasting life," although Jarry slyly suggests otherwise in his essay.

7 Published in *La Revue blanche*, 1 June 1901 (*O.C.*, 2: 620), in which Jarry quotes the author as demonstrating that "the system of Copernicus is as erroneous as that of Ptolemy." "The earth, says she, no more turns around the sun than on itself, but describes each day from west to east, against it, the sidereal circle of which the line of the zodiac is the exact reproduction. This relatively limited orbit forms a mobile center around which circles the moon which for this reason we take for its satellite." From 1901 to 1933, Mrs. Veuve (Fanny) Pierrel published a series of booklets with such titles as: *For Science: Refutation of the Copernican System* (1904); *Triumph of Urania: The Center Earth* (1913; "Urania" is the name of Mrs. Pierrel's system); *Scientific Heresy, We are Misled...the Earth Does Not Turn Around the Sun* (1926). Jarry surely recognized her descriptions as addressing the entirely imaginary concept, rooted in naked-eye perception and intuition, of a "celestial sphere," with a tripartite mythological universe rooted in the idea of the "dry earth" as represented by the "plane of the ecliptic." This tripartite universe, with an "above" described in terms of celestial "hangings" in the "air," and a "below" described in terms of "drownings" (or *settings*) in the "waters below," is the "supplementary universe" of Jarry's pataphysics, as well as that of many other artists and poets.

mytho-cosmological allusions to a *flat earth*, as determined by the "four corners" or "cardinal points" of the locations of the solstices and equinoxes on the ecliptic plane, pierced through the center by a "world axis" (as in Pieter Brueghel the Elder's painting *Land of Cockaigne*, which your lecture of 8 April 1902 suggests that you may know),[8] and for which such mythological "world trees" serve until they are chopped down by a "Man with the Axe" (as in your poem "after and for" Mr. Gauguin and his painting of a similar name) such as your Gaulish Celtic mythological personage named Èsus.[9] This chopping down of the "world axis," which then causes the "starry houses" of the gods to collapse in a *Ragnarok* or "Twilight of the Gods" at the end of each World Age is always followed, as you know, with their being rebuilt by a celestial smith while we *dream* (cf. the *Ubique* epigraph to your *Ubu Enchaîné*).[10] I will not insult your obvious intuitive intelligence here, but will only say that I have recognized in this name of Èsus, as you apparently have, the source of another mythological figure who *hung wounded* from such a *symbolic* "tree" (or *nail*, as you have noticed, as with Odin in the *Veraldar nagli* of Yggdrasil), like the Welsh Celtic Lleu Llaw Gyffes in the *Mabinogion*, and whose name appears many times in the New Testament.[11] But I digress…

---

8 "Le Temps dans l'art," *O.C.*, 2: 637.

9 "L'Homme à la Hache," *O.C.* (1972), 1: 210. The name of this mythological personage appears above his portrait on the first-century CE marble Romano-Celtic "Paris Altar" at the Musée des Thermes in Paris, in which he is shown axe in hand, about to fell a tree. Gauguin's painting is entitled "L'Homme à la hache," and Jarry's capitalization of the final word is significant.

10 *O.C.*, 1: 427. "Cornegidouille! Nous n'aurons point tout démoli si nous ne démolissons même les ruines! Or je n'y vois d'autre moyen que d'en équilibrer de beaux édifices bien ordonnés." ("We will not have demolished everything if we don't demolish the ruins as well! Now I see no other means of doing this than by balancing them with beautiful, well-ordered edifices.")

11 See Waldemar Deonna, "Les Victimes d'Ésus," *Ogam* 10 (1958), 3-29, especially section "5. -*La suspension à l'arbre*," 9.

Upon this *mound* stands a player called the *pitcher*, who faces toward one of the bases, that which is designated *home plate*. Here, on either side of this plate, depending upon his preference, stands a batter holding in his hands the narrow end of a tapered piece of wood that has been turned on a lathe, usually made of *ash*, and which is called a *bat*. I sense your eyes growing rather wide at this juncture, and while it is likely that its name does derive from the French word *batôn*, and although this bat does indeed have a *knob* at the narrower end, it does not *bound* of its own *free will*, the batter instead swinging the bat at a small *ball* (hence the second syllable of the name of the game) about the size of a fist, thrown (or *pitched*) toward home plate by the pitcher. This ball is made of two leather strips (similar in shape to a number 8, and another similar symbol with which you are familiar: ∞), sewn together around a ball of tightly wound twine, comparable to the ancient Roman *harpastum*, itself derived from the Greek *harpaston*, as I'm sure you know. The pitcher thus tries to throw the ball with such speed that the batter is unable to swing the bat in time to hit it (i.e. a *fastball*), or throws a slower pitch to a batter anticipating a faster one (i.e. a *changeup*), or tries to maneuver the ball by causing it to spin (allowing for the effects of aerodynamics on the ball's seams), resulting in pitches known by such colorful names as *slider* or *curveball*. (There is also a pitch called a *knuckleball*, which does not spin at all, but which seems to *float* through the air toward the batter, and which is so difficult to hit that it usually makes the batter look like a *knucklehead*.) This spinning motion (the pitcher may also *whirl* somewhat on the mound in the motion of his delivery, usually on *one leg*, the other pulled up much like the stance of a *crane*) causes the ball to *dance* slightly in its flight toward the batter, making it more difficult to hit. The use of foreign substances, such as that used to throw a *spitball*, is prohibited.

The object of the game is for one team to score more *runs* than the other. This is accomplished by the batter hitting the ball thrown by the pitcher into an area away from any of the fielders. Ideally, the batter will hit the ball so hard that it flies *beyond the outer limits* of the outfield, an act known as hitting a *home run*. This phrase is something of an aberration in that once a player has made such a hit, he does not have to run at all, but may trot or even walk around the bases, unmolested by the fielders, *in a counter-clockwise direction*, until he returns to home plate, thus scoring a run. Judging from your article published in *La Plume* of 15 March 1903,[12] the idea of sending a gleaming white *sphere* as far into *space* as one can with such a *batôn* would not escape your interest. If, however, the player does not hit a home run, but only hits the ball into an area devoid of fielders, he may run only as far as the base that he may reach safely without being "tagged out," or touched with the ball by one of the fielders. From there he can only hope that a subsequent batter will drive him home by means of another hit (again, *ideally*, a home run). If, however, he fails to hit the ball away from the fielders, they may in turn either catch the ball before it touches the ground, or field the ball and throw it toward the base that the batter (now a *runner*) is approaching, where another fielder can then tag him with the ball, either method resulting in what is called an *out* (if there are runners behind him he does not need to be tagged; this is called a *forceout*). *Three outs* constitute the end of the offensive team's half of an *inning*, of which there are, once again, a total of *nine*. This term, much to your dismay I'm sure, has nothing to do with inns, nor with St. Gertrude, nor Siduri (although the playing of baseball often involves the consumption of tremendous amounts of beer, but most often by the spectators rather than the players themselves), nor does it seem to be the reciprocal to the out; the word appears to be a *neologism* of some sort. At any rate, the team with the most runs after nine innings emerges victorious. In case of a tie, extra innings are played.

---

12 "La Méchanique d'"Ixion,"" *O.C.*, 2: 405-407.

Now if you are still with me, as I think you are, here comes the aspect of the game that I think may appeal most to your prodigious imagination: the game seems to take place entirely *outside of time*. In other words, a timeclock has no place in the game of baseball. Certainly an agreed upon starting time is arranged, and yet this can be something as simple as *high noon*, for which one would hardly need a clock to determine. Each half-inning is played until there are three outs, regardless of how long a timespan this takes (the average length of time for a game of baseball again being approximately *three* hours). In the past, games were sometimes "called" on account of darkness, but the game was then resumed the following day. Now, of course, due to the genius of our own Thomas Edison, huge stanchions surround the field with hundreds of electric lights that serve to illuminate it at night, so that the game can continue into the wee hours of the morning if necessary. As practised by many American children however, this absence of timeframe is often extended to include the end of the game as well, there being no regard for either scorekeeping or the counting of innings; it is played, as Heraclitus suggested in regard to time, *with no purpose* beyond the play itself.

There are, of course, many other nuances of the game that can hardly be mentioned in a brief letter such as this (the concept of "strikes" and "balls," and of "walks," for instance); one that I think you would also find of interest is that a runner may *steal* bases. But the use of this term is too complicated to explain briefly; suffice it to say that it is hardly the case of a Prometheus stealing fire from the gods, and more in terms of a Till Ulenspiegel (as in your essay of 1 December 1902,[13] a masterful evocation of the world axis as a "post"[14] which *moves around* depending upon the location of the *perceiver*, a pole star always overhead regardless of where one stands on the planet, due to the tilt of its *axis*) stealing away from the clutches of a shopkeeper whose *andouille* he has just liberated by some cunning means.

---

13 "Les Poteaux de la Morale," *O.C.*, 2: 386-387.
14 See the reference to Hamlet's curious examination of the "post" in the letter signed by eleven writers and artists *O.C.*, 1: 1031-1032.

I hear from a Parisian correspondent that you have been ill; surely with one so young this is simply a case of "spring fever" (cf. here the delightfully illustrated sketch by you and Mr. Bonnard in *Le Canard sauvage*, 21 March 1903).[15] In closing, I wish you the best with your writing career, and look forward to more of your columns, novels, and plays for many years to come.

(signed),

Brisbane di Milo
Cooperstown, New York
USA

P.S. It is customary, in this country, to signal the end of a letter with the word "Sincerely," but having read the "Lintel" to your book of poems on art,[16] I am well-aware of what you think of *sincerity*. A *clair-voyant* (or "sibyl") has tried to tell me that your phrase "anti-aesthetic," employed in "Lintel" in respect to such sincerity,[17] will be co-opted later in this century by a writer named Foster,[18] in regard to something called *postmodernism*, which has nothing to do with either the above-mentioned "posts," nor the kind of *culture* that you address in your book ("*notre* art et science"); she claims that his sense of the phrase is entirely *Baumgartean*,[19] and bears no resemblance whatsoever to your usage, which is clearly, as with so many of your allusions, purely Greek in nature.[20]

---

15 "Soleil de Printemps," *O.C.*, 2: 410-411.

16 "Les Minutes de sable mémorial," *O.C.*, 1: 171-173.

17 "...sincérité, anti-esthétique et méprisable." 172.

18 Hal Foster, ed., *The Anti-Aesthetic: Essays on Postmodern Culture* (Seattle: Bay Press, 1983).

19 Robert Dixon, *The Baumgarten Corruption: From Sense to Nonsense in Art and Philosophy* (London: Pluto Press, 1995).

20 Aesthetic > Gk. *aisthetikos*, of sense perception > *aistheta*, perceptible things > *ais-thenasthai*, to perceive (Webster).

Parts from The Zero's Wedding

Ric Royer

Recently it has been brought to my attention that the science of fourth-dimensional existence has been sectioned off into numeric categories. Like 1 through 7 or 34%. It is my belief that this categorization is a terrible inconvenience. Remember how quick France was in proving that anti-matter actually does have a place in legitimate science? Then how soon was America to conceive the notion that anti-space was an actuality as well? Therefore, America provided us the possibility that France may not even exist at all. A curious existential tyranny.

I can't see stars because I'm being held by the back of the neck. Tonight I will be a balcony. Tonight I will give you my opinion. If I concern myself with matters of the fourth dimension my music might become so complicated that even the Japanese can't play it. For mice, being eaten is the worst that can happen; for humans, it hurts to see friends with new friends.

Take one more example:

I just moved my neck. This was not a reaction to anything but my "Luzcot".[1] By 4 years old, we are already in creative decline.

---

1 Industrial langue: One may not explain himself if he cannot explain himself.

Duchamp's Infrathin

Cal Clements

> The warmth of a seat
> (which has just been left) is
> infra-thin.
>
> —Marcel Duchamp[1]

The concept of infrathin appears in notes that Marcel Duchamp wrote in French during the 1930's and 1940's. These notes were found posthumously in 1968 among other notes from diverse periods. Duchamp's spelling of "infrathin" has several variants: "infrathin," "infra thin" and "infra-thin." It is used occasionally in the plural. Duchamp uses infrathin as an adjective or noun although he states that, since it has no substantive quality, it should be used only as an adjective.[2]

"Infra—" designates below or underneath. It points to something under or slightly outside of normal perception—not unlike the infrared or the infrasonic. "—thin" keeps its standard meaning of narrow or

---

1 Marcel Duchamp, *Marcel Duchamp, Notes,* trans. Paul Matisse (Boston: G. K. Hall and Company, 1983), note 4. Matisse's edition assigns numbers to the notes, but has no pagination. Thus further citations will refer to the note numbers in this edition.
2 Ibid, note 5.

small in depth but adds a (non-scientific) human quality to the term as would "—slim," "—slender," or "—lean."[3]

The infrathin is a call to heightened perception. It is only with special organs that one would be able to distinguish "when the tobacco smoke smells also of the mouth which exhales it," or sense the "separation between the detonation noise of a gun (very close) and the apparition of the bullet hole in the target—(maximum distance 3 to 4 meters)."[4] "Smells," a poorly developed organ in humans, are "more infrathin than colors."[5]

Beyond more sensitive organs, there is a desire to generate new organs completely, innovative sensing machines.[6] One is needed to sense "infra thins [that] are diaphanous and occasionally transparent."[7] It would work like the X-ray machine: "X-rays (?) infra thin Transparency or cuttingness."[8]

---

3 Thus it is fair to translate the French term *inframince* as "infrathin" or "infraslim." Duchamp states that he "chose on purpose the word slim which is a word with human, affective connotations and not an exact laboratory measure." Marcel Duchamp, *The Writings of Marcel Duchamp*, ed. Michel Sanouillet and Elmer Peterson (New York: Da Capo, 1973), 194. Duchamp was himself thin. To be trim through all the ages of life requires a conscious effort to quit eating before getting full. The infrathin may therefore correspond to a feeling of hunger or desire. The infrathin has an erotic dimension. Duchamp associates it with caresses as well as "slippery soap" and "sliding friction." Duchamp, note 28: "Infrathin /caresses" and, for its frictionless quality, note 39. The most overt erotic indication is Duchamp's example of the infrathin as a "female measuring instrument *(sketch)* you cut and you insert the thing." Duchamp, note 19. The sketch that accompanies this note depicts scissors about to cut a sheet of paper.

4 Duchamp, notes 11 and 12.

5 Duchamp, note 37.

6 If the infrathin requires special devices for access, those who have these instruments will be "in the know." Yet the infrathin subverts authority-producing systems. "Inhabitants" of his concept are "do-nothings" through being willfully unproductive. Duchamp, note 34.

7 Duchamp, note 32.

8 Duchamp, note 23.

X-rays, discovered by Wilhelm Conrad Röntgen in 1895, demon-
strate that there is more to the world than what is available to the senses;
by exposing the insides of organisms, they make clear the inadequacy of
human organs to depict all of reality.

> The extrasensory reality revealed by x-rays pointed to
> the most important lesson to be drawn from Röntgen's
> experiments: the inadequacy of human sense percep-
> tion. The popular articles announcing the discovery
> bore titles such as "The World Beyond Our Senses" and
> often included diagrams illustrating the fraction of the
> spectrum represented by visible light versus the much
> greater range of ultraviolet and infrared radiations on
> either side...That x-rays should have interested artists of
> the early twentieth century who were seeking to move
> beyond Impressionism's devotion to visual sensation is
> not surprising. Röntgen's discovery dealt a powerful
> blow to traditional sense-oriented positivism and to
> materialism in general.[9]

X-ray photography gives tangible proof that much more exists in
reality than can be naturally seen. Duchamp, aware of the limits of "reti-
nal art," would see in the X-ray a challenge to realistic representation.

Secondly, X-rays intimate an ability to see the three-dimensional
world *from the perspective of the fourth dimension*. Four-dimensional
vision is often thought to be clairvoyant, meaning that both the insides
and the outsides of things are seen simultaneously and/or that things

---

9 Linda Dalrymple Henderson, "X Rays and the Quest for Invisible Reality in the Art
of Kupka, Duchamp, and the Cubists," *Art Journal* 47 (Winter 1988): 325-6.

blocked by great distances are seen as if nearby.[10] These are qualities that a three-dimensional eye has in viewing a plane and thus ("by analogy") qualities that a four-dimensional eye has in viewing space.

Duchamp connects the X-ray to "cuttingness" since an opaque material, when cut thin enough, becomes diaphanous: "Depending on the material employed the infrathin produces computable transparencies by an increasingly bright beam of light as the material goes from animal to vegetable and to mineral…"[11] It may be that Duchamp wishes to build a machine that would see inside bodies through dissection into infrathin slices, then the exposure of the slices by a bright light, and finally the compiling of the 2d views into a becoming-transparent of the 3d body.

Duchamp defines the assembly of cuts into a higher dimensional form as elemental parallelism.

> Elemental parallelism: repetition of a line equivalent to an elemental line (in the sense of similar at any point) in order to generate the surface. Same parallelism when passing from plane to volume: Sort of parallel multiplication of the n-dim'l continuum, to form the n + 1 dim'l continuum. The process by parallelism is a posteriori. Indeed: knowing the 3-dim'l world, we have, starting from the point, drawn the line by means of elemental parallelism; from the line, by means of elemental parallelism, we have constructed the

10 "A 2-space 'man' inhabiting a plane would see only the lines bounding the 'solids' (plane figures) of his world. A 3-space man sees the enclosed surface as well as the boundaries of such 2-space 'solids' perceiving them to be not really solids but boundaries or cross-sections of the solids of *his* world—the things which he knows to be 3-dimensional, but of which he can see only the outside—By analogy from a 4th dimension these same solids would in turn appear transparent and be perceived to be but boundaries or cross-sections of 4-dimensional solids—clairvoyant vision is of this order, indicating that it is 4-dimensional. Seen clairvoyantly, the internal structure of the human body is visible within its casing, also the aura, or higher-dimensional body." Claude Bragdon, "Man as Seen by Clairvoyant (4-Dimensional Vision), and by Ordinary Human Sight," *A Primer of Higher Space (The Fourth Dimension)* (Rochester, NY: Manas Press, 1913), Plate 19.

11 Duchamp, note 11.

plane, and thus from the plane to the volume. But this
operation already assumed the knowledge or intuition of
the 3-dim'l world. Therefore:
Will the passage from volume to 4-dim'l figure be produced through parallelism? Yes. But this elemental parallelism being a geometric process requires an intuitive
knowledge of the 4-dim'l continuum.[12]

Here Duchamp works with lower dimensional objects to show how
they increase dimensionality. A line is a series of points, a plane is a
series of lines, a cylinder is a series of circles. Using the principle of analogy, one may assume that higher dimensions will relate to one another
in the same way that lower dimensions do. Just as 2d slices can be made
of a 3d solid (the cuttingness of the X-ray), so 3d cuts could represent a
4d form. The process is delayed by the need for an intuitive understanding of 4d forms. In other words, there are *indefinite* ways in which 3d
matter may be configured into 4d shapes. Just as a Flatlander[13] would
understand an unfolded cardboard box, we 3d people can comprehend
a hypercube spread out in three dimensions (cubes in a pattern not

---

12 *The Writings,* 92.
13 Flatlanders are inhabitants of Edwin A. Abbott's *Flatland.* First published in 1884, this
"romance of many dimensions" features Square as the initially closed-minded citizen
of a completely flat world. Square encounters what seems in Flatland to be a circle. Yet
this is a very strange circle since it can perform such feats as shrink and expand at will,
disappear, see through solid objects and speak with a disembodied voice. This visitor
claims to be a Sphere, which is an absolutely impossible and incomprehensible entity
to Square, a Flatlander. In order to prove the existence of Spaceland, the Sphere must
drag Square into the third dimension. Our hero is awe-struck by this spiritually understood revelation (Abbott expresses the event in religious terms) but is quick to extrap-
olate from this experience the existence of even higher dimensions. "As you yourself,
superior to all Flatland forms," Square says to the Sphere, "combine many Circles in
One, so doubtless there is One above you who combines many Spheres in One
Supreme Existence, surpassing even the Solids of Spaceland." Edwin A. Abbott,
Flatland (New York: Penguin Books, 1984), 141. The Sphere is highly offended by such
a blasphemous idea and tosses the Square back into Flatland where, reciprocally, it is

unlike a cross,[14]) but we can't imagine how it folds back into the fourth dimension. The problem is similar to envisioning a finished house on the basis of a set of blueprints—if one has never seen a house before. If the blueprints don't state how the floors will be stacked, the chances of properly composing the floor plan, much less visualizing the final home, will be small. Or, to shift to another example, in the case of a sphere one wouldn't know that the many 2d discs add up in an order that ascends in size and then descends. Unknown 3d "spheres" might start with all the smallest circles and move to the widest, creating a shape more like a funnel. This is where "intuitive knowledge" is needed.

Elemental parallelism is problematic without the infrathin. If the discs, for example, were truly two-dimensional, they would have no height (if positioned horizontally) and thus, similar to shadows, no amount of stacking would ever produce height. In order to form a sphere, one would have to place each 2d circle slightly above the circle below it. The discs would float parallel to each other. Such a disc observed exactly from the side would be invisible. A certain amount of goodwill, imagination, or infrathin on the part of the viewer is needed to fill in the gaps between the floating slices.[15]

---

blasphemous to speak of Space. Abbott's work defends the idea of higher dimensions by showing how minds of a lower dimension will interpret the phenomenon of higher dimensions in terms of common-sense conception of geometry. A standard Flatlander, then, regards talk of Space as insane unless actually taken there. Abbott uses the trope of analogy to "sanely" argue for the existence of higher dimensions. Just as a Flatlander only senses two-dimensional things, we only sense the third dimension; just as most Flatlanders are ignorant of Spaceland, we are ignorant of "the more dimensionable Dimensionality."

14 See Salvador Dali, *Crucifixion (Corpus Hypercubicus)* in the Metropolitan Museum of Art, Chester Dale Collection, 1954.

15 Duchamp may be referring to these sorts of stacking problems when he notes, "While trying to place 1 plane surface precisely on another plane surface you pass through some infra thin moments." Or he may be referring to a perfect alignment of the edges, given that the plane surfaces are of nearly identical shape. Duchamp, note 45.

There seem to be two approaches to the infrathin's thickness in Duchamp's notes. One is to attribute to it a tiny measurement. The other is to give it none.

1. The infrathin can be defined as that which *in a 3d world* is so thin that it is nearly two-dimensional.[16] "Pastel of dandruff fallen from the hair onto a paper wet with glue."[17] Duchamp also speaks of the width of a sheet of paper: "Hollow paper (infrathin space and yet without there being two sheets)."[18] The "hollow" of a sheet of paper may refer to the space between its front and back sides or it may mean a slight depression in the paper.

Duchamp locates the infrathin in thin paper and disqualifies cardboard.[19] Cardboard is less than subtle, being composed of three sheets of thick paper and involving the structuring of the third sheet of paper which repeatedly curves between the straight sheets, thereby giving the material extra rigidity. Ah! A clue. The infrathin involves scale considerations: it is what is slender to the human eye or to the eyes of those smaller than ourselves but what giants might regard as infrathin (cardboard) doesn't count.

The infrathin also concerns the measurement of these minute thicknesses. In note 11 Duchamp gives himself the following task:

---

16 Duchamp's location of higher dimensions in the infinitesimally small may be exactly where such dimensions reside. At the beginning of time, according to the superstring theory of physics (Kaluza-Klein theory), the universe extended itself in ten dimensions but as it cooled six of these dimensions curled up on themselves so that now we notice only time and three spatial dimensions. "[T]he size of these curled up dimensions is called the Planck length, which is 100 billion billion times smaller than the proton..." Michio Kaku, *Hyperspace: A Scientific Odyssey through Parallel Universes, Time Warps, and the Tenth Dimension* (New York and Oxford: Oxford UP, 1994), 16. These strings are too small to be detected by even the largest particle accelerator.

17 Duchamp, note 20.

18 Duchamp, note 17.

19 Duchamp, note 19: "Hollow paper /infra thin space / letter paper not cardboard."

find out in which trade one uses
instruments to measure thickness. (sheet copper
dealers) which go to what
thinness?? 1/10 mm. = 100 μ = thinness of papers

It is important to handle the infrathin with precision. Just as we need special organs to sense the finer infrathin, we need special instruments to measure it and special symbols to talk about it (μ).

"Hollow" *(creux)* paper (from note 19 above) could also refer to a slight depression in an otherwise flat sheet of paper, thus signifying the slightest extension towards an alternative (non-horizontal) direction. Depressions in paper can be used as a model for the shape of space: the general terrain of space is thought by relativity theory to have irregularities caused by massive objects (black holes, dwarf stars, etc.) In this spatial topology, the laws of Euclid no longer hold: angles of triangles can have less (or more) than 180 degrees; parallel lines can eventually meet. The infrathin thus subverts what were once considered self-evident laws of geometry. Duchamp applies such radical analysis to arithmetic as well: "70 + 40 make more than 110—(through infra-thin)."[20]

2. Infrathin also refers to absolutely flat and thin two-dimensional objects to which infrathinness of the first sort (above) must be added if

---

20 Duchamp, note 41. Note also that Dostoevsky champions non-Euclidean mathematics as well. In *Notes from Underground,* the narrator rebels spitefully against scientific determinism which is represented by the formula, 2 x 2 = 4: "Two times two makes four—why, in my opinion, it's mere insolence. Two times two makes four stands there brazenly with its hands on its hips, blocking your path and spitting at you. I agree that two times two makes four is a splendid thing; but if we're going to lavish praise, then two times two makes five is sometimes also a very charming little thing." Fyodor Dostoevsky, "Notes from Underground," trans. Michael Katz, *The Norton Anthology of World Masterpieces,* Vol. 2, 6th ed., ed. Maynard Mack (New York: W. W. Norton and Company, 1992), 1145. Like Duchamp, Dostoevsky asserts that a world of self-evident causation "is no longer life, gentlemen, but the beginning of death." Dostoevsky, 1145.

they are to take on higher dimension. The fact that shadows have absolutely no width qualifies them as examples of this variety of infrathin. If such things as shadows are to stack up into the fourth dimension, it is due to something other than their width; it could be time or virtuality. "The possible is an infra-thin…the possible implying the becoming—the passage from one to the other takes place in the infrathin."[21] This type of infrathin superimposes the viewer on the object viewed.

Whether one obtains a thickness of the first or second type, the infrathin functions as a "conductor" between dimensions.[22] If two-dimensional shapes have an infrathin, then three-dimensional objects must also extend ever so slightly into a higher dimension. The 3d infrathin would arise when 3d objects exhibit a tendency towards wider connection: Déjà vu and simultaneous contrast of color,[23] for example.

Shadows are interesting because while they don't stack up into a 3d object, they *betray* 3d objects. By representing the outline of a solid object, they become signs of the fourth dimension.[24] Duchamp considers the infrathin as a process of signification: "the convention of an arrow sign produces an infra thin reaction on the sense of displacement agreed to."[25] But Duchamp seems to have much more in mind when he

---

21 Duchamp, note 1.

22 Duchamp, note 46.

23 Simultaneous contrast of color, a phenomenon observed by E.M. Chevreul, results from eye fatigue. An extended vision of a specific color "wears out" that color while an excessive amount of receptors for its opposite (green for red, purple for yellow, etc.) begin actually to project that opposite color. Thus, if the eye moves from that worn-out color, its opposite is seen with greater intensity. Mark Rothko made great use of this effect. By lingering in one section of a painting of his and only letting the eye drift into other areas when it will, the viewer experiences the freshest and most luminescent of colors. The painting takes on a virtual aspect and cannot be said to be located securely on the wall. Here, then, we have an infrathin: an ever so tangible leaning towards a greater spatiality.

24 Contemporary computer programs allow users to manipulate objects in hyper-space by altering their 3d "shadows." Kaku, 11.

25 Verso of note 9.

considers shadows. In Note 21, we find the following hint: "cast shadow /oblique /infrathin." Oblique light makes the world strange in at least two ways. It emphasizes even the smallest irregularity in a surface. At dawn, for example, one notices cracks in the asphalt of a road that stand out due to the shadows they cast. Secondly, though related, it creates shadows that are longer than the shadows' objects are tall. A five-foot-tall person, for example, walks at dawn with a 20-foot-long shadow. This shadow extends onto the walls of houses passed, into gardens, and onto other people, wandering into places where *the person* would never go, since such a move would constitute an improper transgression of privacy.[26]

The infrathin is represented not only by shadows but by shadow-casters, "sun, moon, stars, candles, fire," who "work in the infrathin."[27] With the sun, Duchamp seems tentative: "A ray of light (sun) /reduced to an infra thin (probably not possible /because of the 'cone')..."[28] Although light has the property of being invisible "from the side" and moving at the rate of time, how can something as obvious as the sun count as infrathin?

Sun that casts light connects to a widespread trope of daylight. In opposition to daylight is nocturnal light, the light that casts shadows. It is possible to explore these two paradigms of light in terms of their contrasting modes of illumination. Daylight works by reflecting light from a light source onto an object. A reflection (or representation) is

---

26 Such attention to a person's shadow forms the program of Jungian psychology. Here the shadow is seen as the repressed aspects of a personality, those aspects of ourselves that we dislike. When one's personal shadow is thoroughly disregarded, it projects itself into the world around. It becomes those people whom we most dislike, those cultures which must be oppressed or exterminated. Like the criminal, for example, who allows the cop to be an upright citizen, the shadow is the 'other' who nonetheless allows the self to have definition. Identity may be read as A is not B, A is not its shadow.

27 Duchamp, note 3.

28 Duchamp, note 24. It may be that a laser beam would solve the problem (of a ray of light forming an ever-widening cone).

then instantaneously collected by an observer. Since the observer is not included in the object of study, daylight may be said to provide objective, scientific, non-pataphysical knowledge. Mechanical light, or daylight brought into dark spaces, alters this paradigm only slightly. Instead of light being broadly dispersed and defining an entire world through which eyes may roam about as they please, light issues from the same location as the seeking eye; it illuminates only the area that interests the eye. It is as if the eyes were headlights—but harmless headlights. The very essence of daylight is its innocence, its attempt to represent an object without altering it in any way, its attempt to see without leaving a trace.

Nocturnal illumination works through connection and contact. In dark-luminous worlds, the boundary between the subject and object must be indistinguishable for knowledge to begin.[29]

Duchamp does not construct an eye to see the fourth dimension by means of reflected light even though he writes that "Light and shade exist for 4 dim'l as for 3, 2, 1."[30] Reflected light generates *appearance,* which is the ordinary way things are sensed as described by psychology manuals. He investigates another way of looking: *apparition*, which seems to mean the mold-as-perception.

The mold is known in 3d through tactile-perception. Eyes of a lower dimension have a wandering-perception of a dimension one step

---

29 In Lacanian psychoanalysis, this is the analyst's discourse, a discourse based on transference. Transference, here, is not so much the projection of a subject-sup-posed-to-know upon the analyst (although that is necessary to get the process going), but rather a link. Scientific objectivity is suspect when the viewer no longer has the benefit of "vision from afar" or distanced viewing. To "touch" means that the viewer has become a part of the object, has become invested in the object, has "gone native," has become corrupted. It is dangerous to know by touching. Contagions of all sorts move via such physical channels.

30 *The Writings*, 89. Duchamp's notes explore many ideas, some more completely than others, with no thorough attempt at a final synthesis. Often these notes are written on the back of gas bills or other already-used sheets of paper.

higher. (In the following, read the superscript numerals as indicators of dimensional complexity.)

> An eye^2 will only have a tactile perception of a perspec-
> tive^3. It must wander from one point to another and
> measure the distances. *It will not have a view of the whole
> like the eye^3.* By analogy: wandering-perception by the
> eye^3 of perspective^4.[31]

Normal objects are seen from many sides by three-dimensional eyes and then compiled via elementary parallelism into a fourth-dimensional vision. Yet tactile exploration poses the same problem mentioned earlier as germane to elemental parallelism: the project requires an intuitive understanding of the completed 4d solid.[32]

The 4d mold wraps around its 3d object, forming the object through inversion. The 4d eye sees the world as *"circumhyperhypo-embraced (as if grasped with the hand* and not seen with the eyes)."[33] In order to encounter the 4d mold, one must handle 3d parts. This places

---

31 Ibid, 88.

32 Consider a two-dimensional being's attempt to see a sphere via wandering-percep-tion. In order to observe the sphere, the Flatlander sees in two dimensions but is allowed to wander in three (which is to say that one can measure distances between each vision of the object: at one o'clock, at two o'clock…or at 1? dimension-three, 2? dimension-three, 3? dimension-three, etc.) Ideally, she would start at the top of the sphere and move to the bottom, charting the constant variations in width; a sphere could then be constructed, though never seen all at once. The problem is knowing *a priori* where the sphere begins and ends and (secondly) knowing that our extradimensional grid is evenly spaced. A sphere, for example, moving through a plane is not obliged to do so at a constant speed.

33 Ibid, 89. Note that it is not enough for a three-dimensional object merely to be seen from all sides—for that yields only a three-dimensional object seen from all sides, not a vision of the fourth dimension.

the viewer *inside* the mold. The viewer no longer has the benefit of vision-from-afar.[34]

Molds have two parts, the *surface apparition* and the *native color.* Surface apparition "is the image in n-1 dimensions of the essential points of this object of n dimensions."[35] An object (Duchamp uses chocolate as an example) is only a shell, a package of information that holds all the relationships that make up the object's external form. Surface apparition is an epistemological breakdown of the object conducted not by a scientist or a philosopher but by a pataphysician. It is sensory evidence that the object exists *before* being compiled into an idea of substance, unity, or coherence.

Native color, the other quality of a mold, is the unchanging color of the object before an external light source comes into play.

> The native colors are not colors (in the sense of blue, red etc. reflections of lighting X coming from the outside)— They are luminous sources producing active colors—i.e. a surface of native-chocolate color will be composed of a sort of chocolate phosphorescence completing the molded apparition of this chocolate object—[36]

> The object is illuminant. Luminous source. The *body* of the object is composed of luminous molecules and becomes the source of the *lighted* objects' substance (e.g. the chocolate emanating is the atomic mold of the opaque chocolate substance having a physical existence *verified* (?) by the 5 senses. The emanating object is the *apparition.*[37]

---

34 The concept of wandering-perception has a parallel in Deleuze's book on Francis Bacon: haptic vision. With the help of Aloïs Riegl, Deleuze traces this form of seeing to the Egyptians. Gilles Deleuze, *Francis Bacon: Logique de la sensation* (Paris: Editions de la Différence, 1981), 79. The haptic vision, or the tactile quality that one sees in Egyptian bas-relief, links the hand and the eye.

35 *The Writings,* 85.

36 Ibid.

37 Ibid, 86.

Luminous objects evade typical models of representation by provid-
ing their own light. *They feed themselves.* On an epistemological level,
the mode of knowing the object is part of the object itself. Objects
decide how they will be depicted.

Molds cast 3d shadows. Just as a 2d shadow-caster forms a shadow by
blocking light, so a 3d shadow-caster forms the object through reversal,
by surrounding the object in the places it is not. And just as the inside of
a shadow is uniform (a field of darkness), so the interior of a molded
object is homogeneous, being composed only of the substance poured in.

Luminous shadow-casters, which transform 3d objects into 2d shadows, are analogous to transformers of 4d forms that mold 3d shadow-
objects. In both cases, only the outside edges have unique definition.
Also, just as the shadow is cast by a specific object, so each 3d object has
its own mold. 4d molds do not churn out identical replicas. In this
sense, our lives are spent in the infrathin *of the fourth dimension,* at the
boundary of our 3d parts where they are surrounded by a 4d mold.[38]
From this perspective, the three-dimensional world is but a slice of an
infinitely larger and more substantial quadridimensional reality. The
deviant, psychotic, artistic, and/or subcultural members of society
break out of the normative box (3d) to view things from an anamor-
photic angle, a vantage slightly to the side (4d).[39]

---

38 Craig Adcock, *Marcel Duchamp's Notes from* The Large Glass: An N-Dimensional
   Analysis (Ann Arbor: University of Michigan Research Press, 1981), 54.
39 This belief is not uncommon among those enchanted by hyperspace. It figures in
   Lovecraft's "Through the Gates of the Silver Key: "The world of men and of the
   gods of men is merely an infinitesimal phase of an infinitesimal thing—the three-
   dimensional phase of that small wholeness reached by the First Gate, where 'Umr
   at-Tawil dictates dreams to the Ancient Ones. Though men hail it as reality and
   brand thoughts of its many-dimensioned original as unreality, it is in truth the very
   opposite. That which we call substance and reality is shadow and illusion, and that
   which we call shadow and illusion is substance and reality." H. P. Lovecraft,
   "Through the Gates of the Silver Key," *At the Mountains of Madness,* ed. S.T. Joshi
   (Sauk City, WI: Arkham House, 1963), 441.

It is perhaps this that Duchamp had in mind during construction of
Etant Donnés. Here is a sculpture that can only be viewed from one line
of sight: the peepholes carved in the Spanish doors. From this position,
it casts the perfect illusion of a lush landscape with a solid figure in the
foreground. Yet from any other position, positions denied to any but the
museum attendants, the illusion is shattered. A viewer *with access to the
sculpture from those angles* would see that the figure is actually concave,
the clouds are cotton puffs, artificial lighting and motorized waterfalls
support the scene. The properly proportioned world (3d), then, is but a
glimmer of a much vaster and stranger four-dimensional space.

There seem to be three philosophical conceptions of higher space: to
see the beyond as absolute and more real than what is known, to see the
beyond as irreducibly manifold but less real than our world, and to see
the beyond as irreducibly manifold and equally real to our world. The
first path is taken by Plato in his parable of the cave-dwelling shadow-
watchers. The higher dimension is the realm at the outer limit of the sky
that the gods relish in detail while the best souls (philosophers and
lovers) catch a glimpse of it. The rest of us "feed on semblance."[40] The
second approach reverses Plato. The 3d world is clearly apprehended
(in daylight) while the beyond is a delusion. For the post-
Enlightenment world, this position is common sense. The third outlook
stands at a perpendicular angle to the first two. Pataphysics regards
semblance as the only possible foundation while discrediting unity,
truth, and transcendental form as the spin-offs of authority. Reality is
best defined as "epiphenomenona superinduced on phenomenon."[41]

---

40 Plato, *Plato's Phaedrus,* trans. R. Hackforth (London and New York: Cambridge UP,
   1972), 79. Plato's conception survived through the Middle Ages and into the
   Renaissance as Neoplatonism: The 3d world is a stage inhabited by shoddy repre-
   sentations of 4d forms. Scientific rationalism crushed this tradition and forced it
   underground. See Victoria Nelson, *The Secret Life of Puppets* (Cambridge, MA and
   London: Harvard University Press, 2001).
41 Alfred Jarry, *Exploits & Opinions of Dr. Faustroll, Pataphysician,* trans. Simon
   Watson Taylor (Boston: Exact Change, 1996)

The Greek pataphysicians were Sophists who celebrated a rhetorical world where words are as real as the objects they describe. Gorgias argued against the existence of Being while Protagoras held man as the measure of all things.[42]

Duchamp intentionally overlooks questions that ask what is real and what is not; however, it is clear that he doesn't follow Plato. According to Craig Adcock, "Duchamp never argues that the four-dimensional world is more real than our three-dimensional world. He was well aware that the fourth dimensional was less real than the third: it was 'talk'; it was a sophism."[43] This is a curious attribution since it has a positivist Duchamp dismissing the fourth dimension as if it were mere chatter. It is more likely that Duchamp believed that the three-dimensional world is also "talk," hence his statement that "the idea of being is a human invention."[44] The fourth dimension is not "less real than the third," rather reality is transformed at that point into possibility (infrathin). Duchamp can say that the beyond is "talk" or mere sophism while maintaining that, "we content ourselves with the beauty of the mirage, because that is all there is."[45]

Duchamp makes two points that are especially imaginative in relation to the transformation of the normal three-dimensional world into the "continuum." First: "It is certain that every point of space3 conceals, hides, is the end of a line of the continuum. One would like to go around this point and perceive this 4th direction which comes (at this point) into contact with space3."[46] We know that points in our world

---

42 See Gilles Deleuze, "The Simulacrum and Ancient Philosophy," *The Logic of Sense*, trans. Mark Lester with Charles Stivale (New York: Columbia University Press, 1990), 253-279.

43 Adcock, 44.

44 Pierre Cabanne, *Dialogues with Marcel Duchamp*, trans. Ron Padgett (New York: Da Capo Press, 1979), 89.

45 Adcock, 205.

46 *The Writings*, 95.

indicate lines in hyperspace, lines indicate planes, planes, solids, and solids, hypersolids. *How* that line is drawn, however, is unclear; it could slant through the point, meander eccentrically or only begin there.

Second: "Every ordinary 3-dim'l body, inkpot, house, captive balloon is the perspective projected by numerous 4-dim'l bodies upon the 3-dim'l medium. There are 3-dim'l bodies which correspond to fewer perspective projections (in the 4 to 3-dim'l region) than others. One would have to construct/determine those which are the projection of a single 4-dim'l body (4-dim'l perspective)."[47] If one "determines" that all inkpots are projections from a "single 4-dim'l body," interpreted as the Grand Inkpot, this idea reads as Platonic. Yet half of the inkpot could be part of a four-dimensional configuration that also includes the dirt under a potted plant in the garden, the string of a lamp mounted on the ceiling, and the wind created by the spokes of a spinning bicycle wheel.

Duchamp rejects idealism via nominalism. "No more generic specific numeric distinction between words (tables is not the plural of table, ate has nothing in common with eat)."[48] For the nominalist, words are radically incommensurable. Mere transposition in tense is enough to provide differentiation. "Tables" is less meaningful than "table" since each table is not significantly similar to any other table. Even in the singular, "table" is unfortunate since it abstracts and familiarizes the unique event of each table.

> I refuse to think about the philosophical clichés renovated by each generation since Adam and Eve in all the corners of the planet. I refuse to think of it and to speak of it because I do not believe in language, which instead of expressing subconscious phenomena in reality creates thought by and after the word. (I willingly declare myself a 'nominalist,' at least in that simplified form.)

The Writings, 96.
48 Duchamp, note 185.

All this twaddle, the existence of God, atheism, determinism, liberation, societies, death, etc., are pieces of a chess
game called language, and they are amusing only if one
does not preoccupy oneself with 'winning or losing this
game of chess'. As a good nominalist, I propose the word
patatautology, which, after frequent repetition, will create
the concept of what I am trying to explain in this letter by
these execrable means: subject, verb, object, etc."[49]

For the patatautologist, language doesn't represent reality; rather it
generates reality through repetition. If there is something real, it is
under and inside language, in a linguistic subconscious that expresses
itself in failure, death, dreams, and the erotic. Meanwhile the topside of
language creates phantasms (God and his absence, causation and lib-
erty, other linguistic generalizations) that so occupy people's attention
that they rarely experience the indeterminable realities. Thus Duchamp
states that "it would be better to try to go into the infra thin interval
which separates 2 'identicals' than to conveniently accept the verbal
generalization which makes 2 twins look like 2 drops of water."[50]

The infrathin is the world experienced in its irreducible heterogene-
ity. Duchamp's notes on supposed "identities" make this clear. Identities
such as twins, drops of water, and mass produced objects become
infrathin when their difference is noted.

> The difference
> (dimensional) between
> 2 mass produced objects
> [from the
> same mold]

---

49 Marcel Duchamp, *Marcel Duchamp: The Box in a Valise*, trans. David Britt (New
   York: Rizzoli, 1989), 285.
50 Duchamp, note 35 (verso).

is an infra thin
when the maximum (?)
precision is
obtained.[51]

Even if a molded object is identical with another, they differ by being in different regions of space. Furthermore they differ from themselves by being located in separate moments of time. These incongruities make up the essential ingredients of reality. Experience must have a new, sublime element to happen.

Lyotard locates the fundamental alterity of identities in terms of space and time: "each connection of grain to grain must be misrecognizable, alien not only to a different connection between other grains, but to a 'previous' one between the 'same' ones."[52] He argues that avant-garde is that discipline which stresses these metaphysical moments. Lyotard's avant-garde leans upon Kant's sublime. The sublime combines a feeling of pain (due to an inability of the imagination to grasp a phenomenon) with a feeling of pleasure (due to the faculty of reason's ability to understand that same phenomenon).[53] Kant uses the infinite as the exemplar of all that cannot be grasped by the senses (senses feed Kant's faculty of imagination or intuition). Kant's faculty of reason is able to understand the infinite because it can proceed according to formula:

The infinite is the finite + 1.

---

51 Duchamp, note 18.

52 Jean-François Lyotard, *Duchamp's TRANS/formers*, trans. Ian McLeod, (Venice, CA: Lapis Press, 1990), 79.

53 A more contemporary version of the sublime would hold that the sublime is the pain of encountering incommensurable objects combined not with Kant's overarching reason but with an aesthetic, associative, and/or creative act that results in a pataphysical discovery. One collection of these discoveries is Duchamp's definitions of the infrathin.

If Duchamp had spent time with Kant, he, in this writer's opinion, would have dispensed with the faculty of reason. Duchamp prefers the term "indefinite" to "infinite" probably because the former is not a concept. "The term 'indefinite' seems to me more accurate than infinite."[54] It may be that the indefinite is the human version of the infinite, one that has "to be infinite only humanly."[55] Duchamp likes the idea of never arriving but always becoming, as testified to by the art projects worked on for long periods of time. The infinite is too much like a thing already known, a goal reached, a place. Thus we read of the Jura-Paris road:

> Graphically, this road will tend towards the pure geometrical line without thickness (the meeting of 2 planes seems to me the only pictorial means to achieve purity)

> But in the beginning (in the chief of the 5 nudes) it will be very finite in width, thickness, etc., in order little by little, to become without topographical form in coming close to this ideal straight line which finds its opening toward the infinite in the headlight child.[56]

Here we read of an infrathin line that only *approaches* the infinite. Kant's formula to comprehending infinity is bypassed.

Far from embracing over-arching concepts of reason, Duchamp prefers the state of *not even being able to recognize similarity* between two similar objects. He speculates on the loss the ability to recall that item A is similar to item A.

> *To lose the possibility of recognizing 2 similar objects—2* colors, 2 laces, 2 hats, 2 forms whatsoever to reach the

---

54 *The Writings*, 27.
55 Ibid.
56 Ibid.

Impossibility of sufficient *visual* memory, to transfer
from one like object to another the *memory* imprint.

—Same possibility with sounds; with brain facts

At this point, the infrathin is no longer subtle. It marks identical
objects so drastically that they cannot fit the same category. The mark-
ing happens only in the 4th dimension, where the mold of the object
extends.

A Duke Ellington Arrangement

John van der Does

To understand *L'Ecume des jours,* which appeared in 1947 (now out of print but translated as *Mood Indigo* in America and *Froth on a Daydream* in England), it is important to know something about the person who wrote it. Boris Vian was a literary James Dean, an anti-establishment rebel, as well as postmodern Renaissance man. World War II had ended, the Nazi occupation was over, and the caves (cellars made into nightclubs) of the Saint Germain des Pres district of Paris had exploded with creativity. Certainly *L'Ecume* typified that free spirited *apres-guerre* creative force. Jarry defines pataphysics as the science of imaginary solutions, and Jean Baudrillard calls pataphysics the imaginary science of the excess of emptiness and insignificance. *L'Ecume* tells a love story and how the individuals involved get caught in unanticipated excesses and inevitabilities.

In her introduction to *Blues for a Black Cat,* Julia Older, the translator of Vian's short stories, describes Vian as a "pataphysical clown" who refused to compromise or give in to his critics, and yet she goes on: He "produced at least 10 novels, 42 short stories, 7 theater pieces, 400 songs, 4 poetry collections, 6 opera libretti, 20 short story and novel translations; sang on records; acted in films; and wrote about 50 articles on as many subjects."[1] Certainly the book *L'Ecume*, as well as the personality who wrote it, encapsulated the beginning of the postmodern era. Raymond Queneau, one of the most influential figures of modern literature, commented, *"L'Ecume des jours* was one of the poignant love novels of our time."[2] The Existentialist, Jean Paul Sartre, whom Vian pokes fun at in *L'Ecume,* nominated it for the coveted Prix de la Pleiade.

Vian caused two major scandals. He was heavily fined 100,000 francs by the French Government for breaking a law protecting the sanctity of the family caused by his Vernon Sullivan hoax, *J'Irai crasher sur vos tombes* (*I'll Spit On Your Grave*), a novel supposedly written by a black man whom Americans would not touch. The other was his anti-military song, "Le Deserteur," which was forbidden to be aired over French radio waves during the Algerian conflict. Though a light-hearted novel, the same anti-establishment elements found in *J'Irai crasher* and in his anti-war song turn up in *L'Ecume.* Even though *L'Ecume* has been referred to as a fantasy and love story, it can also be described as anti-establishment without being a political novel.

Vian's language swings, but it swings as if written by a seasoned creator. Looking at the annotated French *L'Ecume*, one clearly realizes that the verbal ability of Vian is in the same league as that of Rabelais, Lewis Carroll, Jarry, or Kafka. Mike Zwerin, the translator of *The Jazz Writings of Boris Vian* remarks, "Translating Vian has made me a better writer. He taught me how to approach a serious subject with humor, and how to be seriously humorous. Jazz musicians would benefit from reading Vian. He integrated the physical and the intellectual, the real and surreal, and he swings with words the way a jazz musician ought to swing with notes."[3] *L'Ecume des jours* should be considered a modern day classic.

---

1 Boris Vian, *Boris Vian: Blues for a Black Cat & Other Stories,* ed. and trans. Julia Older (Lincoln and London: The University of Nebraska Press, 1992), ix.
2 Quoted in Jacques Duchateau, *Boris Vian* (Paris: La Table Ronde, 1969), 68.
3 Boris Vian, *Round About Close to Midnight: The Jazz Writings of Boris Vian,* ed. and trans. Mike Zwerin (London: Quartet Books, 1988).

Throughout *L'Ecume*, Vian lets his zany imagination run wild: "The color of the handkerchief was blown away by the wind and settled on a large building or irregular shape, which immediately took the shape of Molitor skating rink."[4] The cook and chauffeur, Nicolas, cannot cook without referring to an edition of *Gouffle*. (Here Vian ridicules the rigid chef, Jules Gouffe, who in 1867 authored a cookbook, the recipes of which have extremely precise measurements.) Recalcitrant neckties refuse to be knotted and fight back. Colin invents a *pianocktail*, a complicated musical instrument that plays melodies which correspond to and produce mixed drinks. Colin and Chloe's marriage turns into a Baroque farce and a jumbled parade of the Religious, the Boodle and the Verjum.

Perhaps a literary giant or perhaps a clown, one wonders why Vian's novels, especially *L'Ecume*, do not enjoy a wide readership. Vian never compromised nor gave into his critics, and he never promoted his own glory. Always with sensitivity and grace, he loved to lambaste society's most cherished institutions: the church, the military, marriage, commercialism, the nine-to-five, five-days-a-week work ethic, and truth—the most imaginary of all solutions. Vian died of a heart attack in 1959 at the age of 39. Many people could never figure him out and quickly dismissed him. During the conservative de Gaulle years, except for a few devoted readers, sales of Vian's books dwindled. Until 1968, his novels—like *L'Ecume des jours*—were considered unfit for study in French schools. However, sales dramatically increased at an extraordinary rate during the Paris uprisings of 1968. '68 was a time when the young French people mistrusted authority. Since '68, a Vian cult has continued to grow.

One of the main themes of *L'Ecume* is unforeseeable tragedy. *L'Ecume* is a love story with a warning: objects of affection do not last

---

4 Boris Vian, *Mood Indigo*, trans. John Sturrock (New York: Grove Press, 1968), 17. Molitor skating rink: a well-known Paris skating rink.

forever. Life appears frivolous, a springtime fantasy. Colin has wealth, many *doublezoons* (money); and he falls in love and marries Chloe. Colin feels awkward; and Chloe, like a Duke Ellington arrangement, appears beautiful, truthful, and outgoing. Both enjoy life. When they walk in the rain down along the Boulevard, their love surrounds and protects them.

Eventually, due to the cost of his marriage and to lending every last *doublezoon* to an ungrateful Chick, Colin is forced to look for work. Colin's love, Chloe, becomes sick: a lily is growing in her chest. Colin has much difficulty finding work but finally gets a job at a munitions factory. His job: to grow rifles by lying on the ground and evenly distributing his body heat so that the rifles will grow uniformly. He is dismissed when flowers appear in the barrels. Colin realizes that the repetitive nature of work relegates everybody to the level of a machine. He wonders why workers believe work is sacred and beautiful and concludes some people avoid thinking and enjoy following routines.

Chloe and Colin had experienced rapturous moments while listening to Duke Ellington's "Mood To Be Wooed." Now Chloe gets even sicker; her room turns in on her and begins to shrink. Chloe dies. Colin no longer has enough *doublezoons* to pay for a proper burial, and Chloe's casket is roughly tossed around. Finally Chloe gets a pauper's funeral on a deserted island. Colin confronts Jesus, pleading that Chloe never did anything wrong in thought and deed, that she was so lovely. Jesus, somewhat bored, adjusts his crown of thorns, and impatiently wants to change the subject. Colin persists adding he invited Jesus to his marriage. Jesus yawns replying Chloe's death has nothing to do with religion.

In 1976 the writer of this article took part in a ten-day Boris Vian colloquium given in Normandy, France, by the Centre Culturel International de Cerisy-la-Salle. There was a French Professor there who did her doctoral thesis on Vian; she compared him to the 400 B.C. Greek Cynic, Diogenes who, back in Grecian times, was considered an utter fool. The Cynics were called "dog-philosophers" because they snarled at pretense, and were antagonistic to all systems which, they felt, were dehumanizing. They reminded the great and powerful to remember their humanity and mortality and to discard all illusions. Certainly Vian, a dropout engineer who easily saw through conventions and facades, must in the Greek sense be considered a Cynic. *L'Ecume des jours*, as well as most of Vian's other works, warns us: enjoy pretty girls and love, but life may turn out differently than anticipated and, above all, mistrust authority.

on languages:

Chris Fritton

28. Was ist 'eine Regel lernen'?—Das.
Was ist 'einen Fehler in ihrer Anwendung
machen'?—Das.
Und auf was hier gewiessen wird, ist etwas
Unbestimmtes.

28. What is 'learning a rule'?—This.
What is 'making a mistake in applying
it'?—This.
And what is pointed to here is something
indeterminate.
—Ludwig Wittgenstein, *On*
Certainty.

what is here
this is here
what is this
this is   retelling
        retelling of what

no, of this
     retelling is here
yes,   retelling is this.

It is not in the self-reflexive nature of thisness
to say thisness is this,
but in this there is a self-reflexiveness
that says this is this.

What is left of this when it is pushed beyond reference?

Contrast.

Contrast is binary
binary is two
this is binary, this is too
this is contrast.

contrast remains after reference
binary is contrast
this is binary
this is contrast
this remains after reference
what is this
this is retelling

what is retelling
retelling is contrast
what is telling
telling is without contrast
this is contrast
this is not telling

there are only two languages
telling and retelling.

this is here
this is retelling
this is contrast
telling is without contrast
telling cannot be this
telling cannot be here.

we can no longer rely on the word
         only   s
and   p
silence   a
                           c
the word is retelling   e
   is not space
    space is not here
  this is not space
    space is not retelling
this is here
this is not silence
here is retelling
silence is not here
silence is not retelling

silence is not retelling
space is not retelling
Silence is Space.
( ) is ( ).
we can no longer rely on this, only space and silence, only telling.

Contributors

Cal Clements (Ph.D., SUNY Buffalo; M.A., University of Georgia; B.A., Emory University) pursues the fourth dimension through writing and objects. His doctoral dissertation was entitled *Cosmic Psychoanalysis: Lovecraft, Lacan, and Limits.* His Master's thesis took the title *Thinking in Four Dimensions: Techniques in Post-Structural Theory for Perception of Hyperspace.* He is currently residing in Athens, Georgia. Questions and requests concerning *Pataphysica* may be sent to cal-clements@yahoo.com

David Daniels' work may be found at www.thegatesofparadise.com and is archived at http://www.ubu.com/; http://ublib.buffalo.edu/libraries/units/pl/collections/manuscripts/index .html; http://www.rediscov.com/sackner.htm. Most recent work includes the Shape Poems in *The Gates of Paradise*: http://www.thegatesof para-dise.com/tgop.htm; http://www.ubu.com/feature/contemp/feature_daniels.html. He is located in Berkeley, California. E-mail: owidnazo@dnai.com

John van der Does studied French, 1972-72, at the University of Besançon, Doubs, France and lived in France for fourteen years. He has been affiliated with the College of Pataphysics since 15 Merdre 103 (June 6, 1976 vulgar era). He took part in a ten-day symposium on Boris Vian held in August 1976 at the International Cultural Center at Cerisy-la-Salle in Normandy and has since continued his interest in the

Vianesque. In 1993 he joined the *Finnegans Wake* Society (Wake Watchers) led by Murray Gross at the Gotham Book Mart in New York. The works of Philip K. Dick, Robert Anton Wilson, George Perec, Joyce, Alfred Jarry and Flann O'Brien continue to arouse his curiosity. Currently he is translating a Vian biography and writing his first novel. He and his wife, Martha Lavender, are building a solar home on ten acres in Vermont. E-mail: mln00p@aol.com

Anthony Enns is a Ph.D. candidate in the department of English at the University of Iowa, where he is currently writing a dissertation on media and mourning in nineteenth- and twentieth-century literature. He has published essays in such journals as *Postmodern Culture, Currents in Electronic Literacy, Studies in Popular Culture, Popular Culture Review, Science Fiction Studies, Quarterly Review of Film and Video, Journal of Popular Film and Television,* and in the anthology *Sexual Rhetoric: Media Perspectives on Sexuality, Gender, and Identity* (Greenwood Press, 1999). He is also co-editor of the anthology *Screening Disability: Essays on Cinema and Disability* (University Press of America, 2001). E-mail: aenns@blue.weeg.uiowa.edu

Chris Fritton studied philosophy and English at SUNY at Buffalo. He is the alumnus editor of *Name* magazine, a venue for undergraduate poetry at SUNY at Buffalo and editor of *Ferrum Wheel* magazine (an assembling that is craftonics, the raw voice of lost and found boxes, poetic parody, the ligaments between art and trash, but most of all, a paper maché bust of William Blake). He has been a participant in BuffFluxus, a group dedicated to determining the exact chemical configuration of the space within a vacuum via event manipulation. He recently finished the book, *Filling Spaces with Heat* (self published) as well as a series of 5 shadow boxes called "The Goddamn Alchemy Project," an organic media non-programmed random transformation from potential to actual and actual to potential; the alchemy of a catalyst causing one to become the other. This is where science cuts off its hands and its lungs fill with fluid, where something secret in nature arranges itself precisely, without aid. He is located on the 3rd floor of 203 Norwood Ave, Buffalo, New York, 14222. E-mail: wirechrist@hotmail.com

Scott Magelssen will begin teaching theatre history at Augustana College, Rock Island, Illinois, in Fall 2002. He received a Ph.D. in Theatre History and Theory from University of Minnesota this spring. He is currently putting together an 8-hour version of Heiner Müller's play HAMLETMACHINE with the University of Minnesota college and theatre practitioner John Troyer. This will be part of the International Federation of Theatre Research XIV World Congress in Amsterdam (July 2002). Recent articles have been published in *antiTHESIS* and *Iowa Journal of Cultural Studies*. Upcoming articles may be found in *Performance Research* and *Journal of Dramatic Theory and Criticism*. Location: Minnesota through July, then Augustana College, Rock Island, Illinois. E-mail: thmagelssen@augustana.edu

MEZ (Mary Ann Breeze) works in the genre of hypertext fiction. It is rumored that she originates from Wollongong, Australia. Her work may be found at http://califia.hispeed.com/RM/mez.htm and other locations on the Internet.

Brisbane di Milo does not exist.

Name: Brian Parshall
Affiliation(s): unaffiliated
Current, recent, imagined projects: respiration
Location: supplementary universe

M. Alejandro Riberi, BA, MA, M.Litt. Researcher at the Hispanic and Latin American Studies, University of Nottingham (UK). Currently working on a research project (PhD) on epistemological aspects in Jorge Luis Borges' narrative fictions. E-mail: aleriberi@yahoo.com, asxmar@nottingham.ac.uk

Ric Royer begins MFA performance studies Baltimore in Fall 2002. He is editor of Ferrum Wheel lit/art project's recent publication *Anthesteria* by bark-art press. Ric may be contacted at pataphysician@hotmail.com. He is currently between Baltimore and Buffalo.

Mark André Singer is Reference Librarian at the Mechanics' Institute Library, San Francisco, California. He recently compiled a selected bibliography on secondary works and adaptations of Shakespeare. He is currently drafting a paper on how to read the word "Dublin" and its variants & permutations in *Finnegans Wake*. Mark imagines a libretto entitled "1453: The Fall of Constantinople". He lives in San Francisco and Appleton, New York. E-mail: markandre_inla@yahoo.com

Index

0-595-23604-9

www.ingramcontent.com/pod-product-compliance
Lightning Source LLC
Chambersburg PA
CBHW030840180526
45163CB00004B/1397